DO ANGELS WALK AMONG US TODAY?

"Do not forget to entertain strangers, for by so doing, some have unwittingly entertained angels."

Hebrews 13:2

Published by Terry J. Boyle
Copyright © Terry John Boyle 2025.

Unless otherwise noted, all scripture quotations are taken from the Holy Bible,
New King James Version Copyright © 1979, 1980, 1982
by Thomas Nelson, Inc.

All rights reserved. No part of this book may be reproduced in any form, stored in a retrieval system, or transmitted in any form by any means—electronic, mechanical, photocopy, recording or otherwise—without the prior written permission of the publisher, except as provided by Australian copyright law.

Words in capitals, or in bold or italics are the emphases
of the author Terry Boyle – terryjohnboyle@bigpond.com

Cover & typeset by Carl Butel at Deep Image – carl@deepimage.net.au

Cataloguing-in-Publication data is available from the
National Library of Australia.

ISBN 978-0-646-71580-3
eBook ISBN 978-1-7642408-0-2

Acknowledgments

I thank my wife, Caroline, for her love, support, and encouragement. I also thank our children Amanda, Felicity, Andrew, Sharon, and their spouses and children for their support.

Our daughter Amanda, for her input, suggestions and encouragement and especially her husband Carl Butel, for the brilliant cover design and internal layout in preparation for printing.

I thank my son Andrew, a Baptist minister, for his input, encouragement, valuable ideas, wisdom, and doctrinal insight.

I thank the leaders of many denominations for their fellowship and input into my life, as well as those associated with A2A over many years.

To all those at Life Ministry Church in Melbourne, where I began ministry, and to all those in Papua New Guinea, where we established a Bible College and ministered as Missionaries for many years. All those at Centre Church in Lismore, NSW, where we ministered for twenty-one years before semi-retiring to the Gold Coast, Queensland, Australia, where we currently enjoy fellowship with several churches.

CONTENTS

Introduction

Quote: Max Lucado

1. Christ our Saviour and Lord
2. Are angels myths, or do they exist?
3. Angels and all the heavenly hosts
4. Angels among us as strangers
5. Angels as ministering spirits
6. Assisting God in answering prayer
7. The fall of Satan and his angels
8. Angels desire to look into the gospel
9. False angels can deceive us
10. Angels used in times of judgment
11. How do we compare with angels?
12. Angels as providers and protectors
13. Are angels church spectators?
14. The Holy Spirit reigns over all angels
15. An angel rolled the stone away
16. The role of angels at Christ's return

Introduction

This is now my seventh book. After completing my sixth book, "Seems like a Good Idea," I told my son Andrew, "That's it; I've finished, no more books." He replied, "Dad, seven is the perfect number; you must do at least one more." So, here we go again! After all, it did "Seem like a Good Idea."

Why write about angels? After reading about a possible encounter with angels in one of my other books, our good friend Trish said, "Why not do a book on angels?" Anyway, I have always been fascinated by biblical encounters with angels.

But do they still walk among us today?

"Do not forget to entertain strangers, for by so doing, some have unwittingly entertained angels." Hebrews 13:2.

Upon examining the context of this scripture, it becomes clear that it refers to the church's responsibility to demonstrate love and acceptance to everyone, including strangers. It also implies that some strangers may be angels in disguise.

My wife and I are convinced that angels have appeared to us as strangers in human form on several occasions to help, guide, and direct us when we needed it most. I will share some of these remarkable encounters and other possible angelic stories we have experienced throughout this book.

On one occasion, after a prayer meeting, I had a strange experience that I attribute to an angel, which I will share in detail at some stage in this book. I have been aware of angels, sensed their presence, and been very thankful for their help and protection over many years in ministry.

I want to explore the origins of angels, their purpose, how they operate, and the circumstances under which we will likely encounter them personally.

Throughout history, people have told incredible stories of how angels have protected and watched over them. Although it may be difficult to authenticate incidents with angels, we must accept that they exist, are real, and have a purpose.

In doing so, I do not want to detract from the sovereignty of God our Father, the great salvation and redemption we can only find in Christ, and the power of the Holy Spirit.

Quote

"When we arrive in heaven, I think we will be surprised to learn how many times angels were involved in our lives, and we never knew it"

Max Lucado

DO ANGELS WALK AMONG US TODAY?

Chapter 1

Christ our Saviour and Lord

"Then the angel said to them, "Do not be afraid, for behold, I bring you good tidings of great joy which will be to all people." "For there is born to you this day in the city of David a Saviour, who is Christ the Lord."

Luke 2:10-11.

In the above scripture, an angel appeared to shepherds living in the fields, watching over their flocks by night, and announced that Christ, the Messiah, had been born.

As we explore the mystery of angels and extol their function and purpose, it must be apparent from the outset that Christ is far superior to any of the angels. He alone is our Saviour and Lord.

Although the Bible describes angels as magnificent beings, none can compare with Christ. He is exalted far above all the angels. The writer of Hebrews describes this, extolling Christ over the angels as our Lord and Saviour.

"God who at various times and in various ways spoke in times past to the fathers by the prophets; has in these last days spoken to us by His Son, whom He has appointed heir of all things, through whom He also He made the worlds; who being the brightness of His glory and the express image of His person, and upholding all things by His power, when He had by Himself purged our sins, sat down at the right hand of the Majesty on high, having become so much better than the angels, as He has by inheritance obtained a more excellent name than they."

Hebrews 1:1-4.

The focus of our salvation and the gospel is now upon Christ, who is exalted far above the angels. The writer of Hebrews clarifies this by stating that God never called any angel His Son or claimed to be their Father.

"For to which of the angels did He ever say: You are My Son, Today I have begotten you." "I will be to Him a Father, and He will be to Me a Son." "Let all the angels of God worship Him?"

Hebrews 1:5-6.

In Mere Christianity, C.S. Lewis says, "A man who was merely a man and said the sort of things Jesus said would not be a great moral teacher." He would either be a lunatic, on the level with the man who says he is a poached egg, or else He would be the devil of hell. You must make your choice." Lewis strongly believes in the uniqueness of Christ, approaching it with a philosophical and imaginative perspective. He argues that Jesus must be Lord, liar, or lunatic, rejecting the idea that Jesus was merely a great moral teacher.

Jesus said, *"I am the way, the truth, and the life." "No one comes to the Father except through me."* John 14:6.

In Institutes of the Christian Religion, John Calvin wrote, "Christ alone is He to whom the Father has committed all power, and to whom alone we must flee for salvation."

When I was saved, I believe the Holy Spirit convicted me of my sin and revealed Christ as my only hope of forgiveness and salvation.

At the age of twenty-three, I responded to an altar call in a small house church meeting, publicly repenting my sins and confessing Christ as my Saviour and Lord. I was born again by believing in Christ. My life changed from that moment.

"If you confess with your mouth the Lord Jesus and believe in your heart that God has raised Him from the dead, you will be saved." Romans 10:9.

However, to come to this point in my life, I am convinced that angels had a part to play, especially in protecting my life from a premature death on several occasions. At twenty-one years of age, I was on a working holiday, miles from my hometown of Horsham in Victoria. I was driving along a remote gravel road from Esperance, Western Australia, to explore Cape Le Grand National Park. One of the world's most beautiful and serene beaches is in this protected area.

I was driving too fast at the time, as I had never been there before and was unfamiliar with the road. I came up a hill to a blind corner and lost control; skidding in the gravel, the car left the road, was airborne, started to roll over, and then suddenly righted itself and seemed to float back to the side of the road.

I sat there in shock, thinking I was going to die as the car rolled over. I was stunned, not hurt, and the car was okay. After a while, I continued my journey. I was not saved then, but I walked along that beautiful beach with its pure white sand and turquoise water, the waves breaking and glistening in the sunlight, and I thanked God for saving my life. As I look back now, I believe angels intervened.

As long as I can remember, I had a deep longing in my heart to know God. I wished I knew more about God. We had a family tradition: when we shared a roast chicken, whoever got the wishbone would make a wish. I would wish for a list of things, but I would always end the list by wishing I knew God.

Although I was a sinner and did not have a religious church background, apart from attending a Presbyterian Sunday School for a few years, but as I look back on my search for God, I am so grateful that He responded to the cry of my heart, revealing His grace and mercy to me and for the silent and unseen ministry of angels, then, and throughout my life and years in ministry.

But do angels walk among us today?

Chapter 2

Are angels myths, or do they exist?

"Bless the Lord, you His angels, who excel in strength, who do His word, heeding the voice of His word."

Psalm 103:20.

The Bible is quite clear that angels exist to serve God. However, to some, angels are no more than mythological creatures or mere superstition.

I realised recently that not a lot is taught about angels. I have lectured at several Bible Colleges in Australia and have been instrumental in establishing a Bible College in Port Moresby, PNG. As far as I can recall, none had a separate or complete subject on angels.

Therefore, I was inspired to conduct more research that helped shape the creation of this book.

Throughout history, most people have widely accepted the existence of angels, but their interpretation of what they are like and what they do varies significantly. It depends on whom you ask!

I will outline some prominent viewpoints frequently expressed regarding the existence of angels and the understanding people seem to have of them.

Are angels just myths or fairy tales?

Some suggest angels are myths or fairy tales intended to comfort and entertain children. They view them as mythological beings, symbolic representations in ancient texts and records that misrepresent natural events.

Many hold to these beliefs; I will quote just two prominent ones.

Carl Sagan, an Astronomer and Scientist, is quoted as saying, "Angels are an idea that originated in the childhood of our species; they are comforting, but there is no compelling evidence for their existence."

Richard Dawkins, a Biologist and Atheist, says, "Angels belong in the same category as fairies, goblins, and leprechauns - charming stories, but not something that belongs in rational discourse."

They may not be supported by objective evidence, but how do those who hold to these beliefs explain how they remain powerful myths that reflect human hopes and the need for comfort and meaning in times of distress and grief? If they are mere myths, how have they profoundly impacted theology, art, ethics, religion, and supernatural events throughout history?

New Age Thinking

New Age practitioners claim that angels serve as guides for personal enlightenment and can be contacted through meditation or prayer. They are not tied to any specific religion but are willing to help everyone. They are guardian spirits that protect people. Intermediaries between God and humans. They are beings of light to help in times of need. Some say they all have wings.

To quote two practitioners who hold to these beliefs.

A New Age practitioner, *Diana Cooper*, says, "Angels are beings of light who love us unconditionally. When we call upon them, they assist us in ways that surpass human understanding.

Gabrielle Bernstein, a New Age practitioner, says, "Angels work through our thoughts, our intuition, and our dreams. When we quiet the mind, we can hear their guidance more clearly."

Although these thoughts may sound reasonable and comforting, they are not supported by scripture and can lead people astray.

Myths, metaphors, or reality

Whether myths, metaphors, or reality, some religious and non-religious people claim encounters with angels and report feeling an unseen presence protecting them, as well as miraculous rescues or warnings of impending danger. Some individuals report seeing beings of light in near-death experiences, while others attribute healings to angels.

Many popular songs today are about angels, whether they refer to supernatural or human angels. Robbie Williams, English singer-songwriter, sings a song called Angels with the opening lyrics –

"I sit and wait, does an angel contemplate my fate? And do they know the places where we go,

When we're grey and old? Cause I have been told,

That salvation lets their wings unfold."

Although some of these songs may be questionable from a theological perspective, they confirm the belief in the existence of angels.

However, some can become cynical in times of tragedy, especially if it involves the death of a loved one. In times of grief, I have heard people say, "Where were the angels?" I thought they were meant to protect us?"

It is hard to give a satisfactory answer to quell their grief, though we must accept that our life and time on earth are in God's hands.

After I retired, I spent some time with Volunteer Marine Rescue (VMR). First aid was part of our training, as we often had to assist people seriously injured in boating accidents or water-related incidents.

I remember an experienced ambulance officer instructing us in first aid and telling us of some of his experiences when attending accidents, how some people with serious injuries should have died but survived, and how others with hardly a visible mark on them were pronounced dead. He then surprised me by saying, "Our life is in God's hands; when our time is up, it's up."

The Bible confirms what he said, that our lives are in God's hands.

"In whose hand is the life of every living thing. And the breath of all mankind." Job 12:10.

The Christian view

Christians view angels as God's messengers. The English word "angel" originates from the ancient Greek word "aggelos," pronounced "angelos," meaning "messenger." In the Old Testament, the equivalent Hebrew word for "messenger" is "malak," also translated as "angel," which refers to a messenger from the Lord in the context.

As outlined below, angels serve multiple functions beyond simply delivering messages to people. I will elaborate on these points throughout the book.

- **Angels worship and serve God.**

- **Angels deliver messages to humans.**

- **Angels minister to Christians.**

- **Angels protect and guide people.**

- **Angels carry out God's judgments.**

- **Angels are spirit beings who do not marry.**

All of the above can be validated by scripture. If you believe the Bible is the word of God, then you must believe that angels exist.

But do angels walk among us today?

Chapter 3

Angels and all the heavenly hosts

"Praise Him, all his angels; Praise Him, all His hosts!....."Let them praise the name of the Lord, for He commanded and they were created."

Psalm 148:2 and 5.

When God created the heavens and the earth, including Adam and Eve, as described in the book of Genesis, the angels and the heavenly hosts were not mentioned in the creation account.

However, the above scripture, along with others that support it, verify that God, at some point, created angels and all the heavenly hosts. It is believed that they did not exist eternally from the beginning, as it is evident that God created them.

According to scripture, Christ is superior to all the angels and heavenly hosts and has been involved in both creations.

"He (Christ) is the image of the invisible God, the firstborn over all creation. For by Him were all things created that are in heaven and that are in earth, visible and invisible, whether thrones or dominions or principalities or powers. All things were created through Him and for Him." Colossians 1:16.

As a member of the Trinity, Christ, the Word, or the Son of God, existed from the beginning. So, we will begin with Christ and work our way through the heavenly hosts, including the hierarchy of angels.

Christophanies

These are Old Testament references to the "Angel of the Lord." Some, but not all, are considered pre-incarnate appearances of the Lord Jesus Christ (Christophanies) and are often identified with God Himself. Depending on how we interpret them, they can sometimes be difficult to discern.

For example, Sarah clashed with Hagar, her maidservant. So, Hagar had fled from her presence, and the "Angel of the LORD" found Hagar by a water spring in the wilderness.

"The Angel of the LORD said to her, *"Return to your mistress; and submit yourself under her hand....."* "Then she called the name of the LORD who spoke to her, You-Are-the-God-Who-Sees; for she said, "Have I also seen Him who sees me?"* (Interpreted by most scholars as a Christophany). Genesis 16:9 and 13.

On one occasion, the Jews challenged Jesus when He implied that before Abraham was, He existed. They said to Him, *"You are not yet fifty years old, and have you seen Abraham?"*

Jesus answered them, *"Most assuredly, I say to you before Abraham was I AM."* John 8:57-58. Jesus was referring to His eternal existence as God in some shape or form.

Why is Jesus sometimes called the *"Angel of the LORD"* in the Old Testament? He was part of the Trinity, comprising the Father, the Son, and the Holy Spirit. He was not ready to be fully revealed as the Son of God until He began His ministry on earth. The apostle Paul speaks of Jesus and the gospel as a hidden mystery that is now revealed in Christ.

What are the living creatures?

They are not just angels; they appear to be in a class of their own. They are portrayed as the living creatures around the throne of God, as described in Ezekiel 1:4-14 and Revelation 4:6-8. They are powerful celestial beings that serve and worship God continuously, but are not directly mentioned as angels.

Both references describe them as having four faces: a lion, an ox, a man, and an eagle. Many scholars believe they symbolise the attributes of God and can be paralleled to the gospels. The Lion - Matthew (Jesus' Kingship), The Ox – Mark (Jesus' Servanthood), The Man – Luke (Jesus, Son of Man), John – The Eagle (Jesus, Son of God).

Cherubim –

They are also called Cherub in the singular. These cherubs are not the popularised little baby-like cherubs depicted on Valentine's Day cards who play harps and shoot arrows through love hearts. Aside from God, these are some of the most powerful beings in the universe, ministering directly before God's throne. They are Considered to be *"Guardians of Glory."* They appear to be guardians of sacred things, protecting God's presence and glory.

"Then the glory of the Lord went up from the cherub, and paused over the threshold of the temple; and the house was filled with the cloud, and the court was filled with the brightness of the Lord's glory." Ezekiel 10:4. For those who wish to investigate them further, Ezekiel chapters 1 and 10 provide detailed descriptions.

There are two other primary references to Cherubim. They were placed to guard the tree of life.

"He placed Cherubim at the east of the Garden of Eden, and a flaming sword that turned every way, to guard the way to the Tree of Life." Genesis 3:24.

They are also mentioned as symbolic gold figures on the mercy seat. *"And you shall make two cherubim of gold; of hammered work, you shall make them at the two ends of the mercy seat"*... *"And the cherubim shall stretch out their wings above, covering the mercy seat with their wings, and they shall face one another, and the faces of the cherubim will be toward the mercy seat."*.... *"And there I will meet with you, and I will speak to you from above the mercy seat, from between the two cherubim which are on the ark of the testimony."* Exodus 25:17-22.

The role of the living creatures is not entirely clear, but they appear to be guarding sacred things and serving and worshipping around the throne of God. They are described in Revelation as having a continuous, non-stop ministry.

"And they do not rest day or night, saying: Holy, holy, holy, Lord God Almighty, who was and is and is to come." Revelation 4:8.

Seraphim –

Considered to be the "Burning or Fiery Ones"

They resemble the living creatures described in Revelation but are only mentioned once in the Bible. There is possibly more than one, with each having six wings: two wings covering their faces, two covering their feet, and two for flying.

"And one cried to another and said, "Holy, holy, holy is the Lord of hosts; the whole earth is full of His glory!" Isaiah 6:3. Their role seems to be leading some form of worship.

They also appear to purge and purify with Holy fire. When Isaiah saw them, he said, "I am a man with unclean lips." One of the Seraphim flew to him with a coal from the altar and touched his lips to purge and take away his sinfulness.

I do not pretend to understand these magnificent living creatures who make up part of the heavenly hosts, which include angels.

Angels have a hierarchy

It would appear that angels have a hierarchy of their own, which I will endeavour to expound.

Archangels – According to some traditional scholars, the scriptures suggest that there were three archangels in the beginning: Lucifer, Michael, and Gabriel. Lucifer fell, taking a third of the angels with him (Revelation 12:4).

However, in Ezekiel 28:14, Lucifer or Satan is called the anointed cherub. Whatever the case, I will elaborate on Lucifer and the fallen angels in a separate chapter. That leaves us with two possible active archangels, Michael and Gabriel, and perhaps Lucifer, a fallen archangel. However, the Bible only refers directly to Michael as an archangel.

Michael – *"Yet, Michael the archangel, in contending with the devil, when he disputed about the body of Moses, dared not bring against him a reviling accusation, but said, "The Lord rebuke you!"* Jude 9.

The Greek word for archangel is archaggelos, pronounced "arch-angelos", which means "chief angel." Does this narrow it down to only one archangel, Michael? However, it is implied in Daniel that Michael came to help deliver a message from God in response to Daniel's prayer.

"But the prince of the kingdom of Persia withstood me twenty-one days, and behold, Michael, one of the chief princes, came to help me." Daniel 10:13.

Notice that it says Michael, one of the chief princes, came to help me. Who did he come to help? This may refer to the existence of another archangel in this context. Therefore, there is a distinct possibility that another archangel exists, most likely Gabriel, the messenger of God, who was bringing a message to answer Daniel's prayer.

Even though Daniel's prayer was heard from the very first day, a spiritual battle raged in the heavens, and it took twenty-one days for the answer to his prayer to reach him. Michael is in charge of the armies of heaven and is a mighty warrior angel who leads other angels and engages in spiritual battles.

"And war broke out in heaven: Michael and his angels fought with the dragon, and the dragon and his angels fought, but they did not prevail, nor was there a place found for them in heaven any longer." Revelation 12:7-8.

Gabriel – He is often referred to as "the messenger of God." No scripture reference calls him an archangel. His name means "mighty one." He is regarded as a powerful angel, possibly another archangel. It is only feasible to have more than one, like an army has more than one general.

Gabriel, in scripture, is undoubtedly the most prominent messenger God uses to convey monumental messages that can change the course of history.

"Gabriel, make this man understand the vision."… "Understand, son of man, that the vision refers to the time of the end." Daniel 8:16 and 18.

When an angel speaks to Zacharias about his wife Elizabeth bearing a child (John the Baptist), He doubts it and says to the Angel,

"How shall I know this? For I am an old man, and my wife is well advanced in years." And the angel answered and said to him, "I am Gabriel, who stands in the presence of God and was sent to speak to you and bring you these glad tidings." Luke 1:18-19.

Zacharias became mute because he doubted, and he could not speak again until after John's birth.

The angel Gabriel was also sent to Mary to announce that she would bear a child, Jesus, the Saviour (Messiah).

"The angel Gabriel was sent by God to a city of Galilee named Nazareth, to a virgin betrothed to a man named Joseph, of the house of David. The virgin's name was Mary." And having come in, the angel said to her, "Rejoice, highly favoured one, the Lord is with you; blessed are you among women."… "And behold, you shall conceive in your womb and bring forth a Son, and shall call His name Jesus." Luke 1:26-27.

Ordinary Angels

The term' ordinary angels' may not be the most appropriate term, as all angels are majestic beings; however, I feel that the lower-ranked angels, or the so-called ordinary angels, are more likely to be the ones we will encounter here on earth today.

There is a song by Craig Morgan called "Ordinary Angels." Some of the lyrics are –

> It could be someone walking down the street
> A stranger on a bus
> A little kid on his way to school
> Or any one of us
> We all got a little Superman ready to take a flight
> And save a life. Oh, save a life
> Take a look around you
> And you'll see ordinary angels

The song probably refers to ordinary people who act or treat us like angels. But it could also refer to any of us or strangers veiled as angels.

The point is that angels are still walking among us today.

How many angels exist?

We do not know, but the scriptures indicate that the number is incomprehensible.

"But you have come to Mount Zion and to the city of the living God, the heavenly Jerusalem, to an innumerable company of angels." Hebrews 12:22.

"Then I looked and heard the voice of many angels around the throne, the living creatures, and the elders, and the number of them was ten thousand times ten thousand and thousands of thousands." Revelation 5:1.

This isn't easy to interpret, as ten thousand times ten thousand equals one hundred million. Then, adding thousands of thousands in the plural form could be in the billions. Perhaps a skilled mathematician could devise an acceptable number.

Whatever the case, they outnumber fallen angels two to one, assuming that Lucifer (Satan) fell with one-third of the angels.

When Jesus was arrested, He rebuked Peter for cutting off the servant's ear with his sword.

"Do you not think I can now pray to My Father, and He will provide Me with more than twelve legions of angels?" Matthew 26:53.

Why twelve legions? Is Jesus thinking of His twelve disciples or the twelve tribes of Israel? A legion of Roman soldiers consisted of approximately six thousand men. Multiplied by twelve would be seventy-two thousand angels.

Imagine what this number could accomplish if one angel could kill 185,000 Assyrians (2 Kings 19:35).

What angels are not!

Contrary to what some believe, they are not -

> *Omniscient* – All-Knowing.
> *Omnipresent* – All-Present.
> *Omnipotent* – All-Powerful.
> Angels are not mediators.
> Angels are not to be worshipped.
> Angels are not married.

But do they walk among us today?

Chapter 4

Angels among us as strangers

"Do not forget to entertain strangers, for by so doing, some have unwittingly entertained angels."

Hebrews 13:2.

Now we begin to answer the question: Do angels walk among us today?

In the context of this scripture, it refers to Christians and churches demonstrating love and hospitality to all, including strangers.

However, the phrase "to entertain strangers" leaves it open for us to speculate as to what that may mean, for by so doing, some have unwittingly (or without really knowing it) entertained angels.

It seems to me that, at times, angels may be among us in human form, as strangers, without our awareness. Maybe you feel the same way?

First, consider an example from the Bible where angels appear in human form. In Genesis 18 and 19, Abraham and Lot encounter the same angels who appear to them as ordinary men. Although they were somehow recognised as angels in this example, the point is that they were described as appearing like men, not obvious angels with wings.

Abraham was sitting at the tent door in the heat of the day when he looked up and saw three men standing by him.

"So, he lifted his eyes and looked, and behold, three men were standing by him; and when he saw them, he ran from the tent door to meet them, and bowed himself to the ground, and said, "My Lord, if I have now found favour in Your sight, do not pass on by your servant." Genesis 18:1-3.

Most scholars agree that the three men are, in fact, the Lord with two angels. They tell Abraham and Sarah they will bear a son in their old age.

After speaking to Abraham and Sarah about bearing a child, the Lord revealed to Abraham that they were about to destroy the nearby city of Sodom, where Lot lived. Abraham began interceding for the city, pleading with the Lord to spare it if there were fifty righteous people; he stopped pleading at ten righteous people. The Lord agreed and said if He found ten, he would not destroy it. However, he could not find ten, so the city would be destroyed.

In the last verse (33) of chapter 18, we read. "So, the lord went His way as soon as He had finished speaking with Abraham, and Abraham returned to his place."

However, in the next verse (19:1), we read, *"Now the two angels came to Sodom in the evening, and Lot was sitting at the gate of Sodom."* (It is thought they were the same two angels with the Lord speaking to Abraham.)

"When Lot saw them, he rose to meet them, and bowed himself with his face toward the ground." And he said, *"Here now, my lords, please turn into your servant's house and spend the night."* …..Now, before they lay down, the men of the city, the men of Sodom, both old and young, all the people from every quarter, surrounded the house. And they called to Lot and said to him, *"Where are the men who came to you tonight? Bring them out to us that we may know them carnally."* Genesis 19:1-5.

The angels must have looked like men, as the men of the city wanted to exploit them sexually. Lot pleaded with them not to do such a wicked thing and instead offered his daughters to them. But as the men of the city came to Lot's door, the angels blinded them so they could not find it. They told Lot to take his family and flee the city before it was destroyed.

When Lot told his sons-in-law, they thought he was joking. But when the morning dawned, the angels told him to hurry, take your wife and daughters and flee from the city.

"For we will destroy this place; because the outcry against them has grown great before the face of the Lord, and the Lord has sent us to destroy it." Genesis 19:13.

That is precisely what happened; they fled as fire and brimstone rained down and destroyed the city of Sodom and Gomorrah.

This may not be the best example, as although they were recognised as angels in this instance, it shows us that angels can appear in human form.

However, in far less dramatic situations, angels can come to us not as obvious angels, but as strangers to help us in times of need because God loves and cares for us.

My wife and I have likely experienced incidents where strangers appeared out of nowhere to help us, and it has led us to wonder: was it just a coincidence, or was it an angel sent from God to assist us in our time of need? You may have had similar encounters.

Several personal encounters

I will share several personal experiences, although I have no way of validating them, I would like to think the strangers in these stories were, in fact, angels on assignment.

Tower Bridge London -

My wife and I were trying to see the key sights of London. We were on a bus and wanted to get off to see the Tower Bridge. I went to the driver to ask him where we should get off the bus. He seemed vague, as his English was very poor. However, a woman sitting opposite us leaned over and said, "Get off when I get off, and I will show you where to go."

We followed her off the bus, and she said, "I'll take you and show you around." She was like a tourist guide, showing us some points of interest, taking us around Saint Katherine's Dock (which we had not known existed), and then across to a statue of a lady with a dolphin. She said, "This is the most popular spot for taking photos of the Tower Bridge."

My wife and I began taking some photos. I decided to take a picture of this lovely lady, but when I looked around, she had vanished. I hurriedly looked for her but could not find her anywhere. We felt later that she could have been an angel.

In the Australian wilderness -

My wife and I were travelling in a rugged, remote area of Western Australia. We had just been to a place called "Python Pool" in the middle of nowhere and were completely alone.

On a stony gravel road heading further east into a deserted area, my wife said, "I think we have a flat tyre." I was in denial as I did not want to stop in the heat in such a remote area. But it became apparent that something was wrong, so I stopped.

When I got out of our Jeep and looked at the back tire, I was horrified; it was ripped to shreds and down to the rim.

We were contemplating what to do when suddenly, out of the blue, a man who claimed to be a ranger stopped behind us and offered to help us. He changed the tyre for us, and then, after examining our other tyres, he strongly advised us not to continue into the wilderness but to head back to Karratha on the coast to get a new set of tyres. It was over 200 kilometres back to the coast, but I reluctantly heeded his advice and went back.

When we arrived back in Karratha, we searched for the right tyres but had trouble finding some suitable for our vehicle until we came across a place that had exactly what we wanted on backorder, which someone had failed to pick up.

We were convinced that man was an angel. We continued our journey the next day and finally reached our destination, the mining town of Tom Price, before moving on further into the outback.

Smuggling Bibles into Myanmar (Burma) -

I was travelling with a fellow minister and friend, Denis Barnard, to minister at a Bible College in Hyderabad, India. The Ministry of Open Doors had contacted Denis to see if we would be willing to divert to Myanmar to smuggle some Bibles into the country.

We landed in Bangkok, where we met a contact who provided us with extra cases to smuggle small, neatly gift-wrapped Bibles into our luggage. We were told it would be dangerous as the country was under strict military rule and was anti-Christian.

That night, I had a nightmare; I dreamt we were caught for smuggling Bibles and stood against a wall to be shot. A soldier offered me a cigarette in the dream, and I replied, "No, thanks; I don't smoke." I woke up in a cold sweat. I prayed, "Lord, give me something to destroy the spirit of fear over me," and Isaiah 41:10 came to mind.

"Fear not, for I am with you; be not dismayed, for I am your God. I will strengthen you; Yes, I will help you; I will uphold you with My righteous right hand."

We flew from Bangkok to Rangoon. As the plane landed, an announcement came over the intercom that everyone's luggage would be X-rayed. I began meditating on Isaiah 41:10.

Armed soldiers were everywhere; all we could do was keep praying. We went through the passport procedure and were directed to take our luggage, containing about thirty small Bibles each, to the X-ray machine.

We were nearly there when a man in uniform suddenly stepped in front of us and escorted us through the exit gate. The Lord had fulfilled His promise to help us. I am convinced that man was an angel. The next day, we delivered the Bibles to an underground church group, which was overjoyed to receive them. The following day, we flew out to India.

On the mission field in PNG -

On one occasion, I travelled with Barry Winton, a missionary in Bougainville. We were going deep into the jungle on our way to a Christian Camp in a remote area. We had to cross several rivers in a four-wheel drive Suzuki. It had been raining, and the rivers were high.

We arrived at the most significant river to cross and hesitated, as it was late in the day, but we decided to try it. We were halfway across when we got stuck. The water was nearly up to the window, and I saw fish swimming around when I looked out.

We were in trouble, so we sat there and prayed. Suddenly, several strong-looking men emerged from the jungle, waded over to us, pushed us to the other side, and then disappeared back into the jungle.

An Angel to the rescue

The Rev. Graham Tomlin, the former Bishop of Kensington, recounts the story of a soldier friend who was in trouble on an army climbing expedition in Kenya. One of his team had fallen to his death from a sheer rock face. Caught up in the moment's drama, he found himself stuck on a ledge, unable to move up or down, paralysed by fear. Suddenly, a climber appeared out of nowhere, moved onto the ledge he was on, tied a rope into his harness, and lowered himself down to safety before disappearing up the face of the mountain, never to be seen again. The soldiers were the only registered group on the mountain at that time. He was convinced it was an angel that rescued him.

Yes, I believe angels walk among us today. I will share other possible encounters with angels in the following chapters.

Chapter 5
Angels as ministering spirits

"Are they not all ministering spirits sent forth to minister for those who will inherit salvation?"

Hebrews 1:14.

Angels are ministering spirits, so they are not readily visible unless God opens our eyes to see them. However, this verse introduces us to the heart of their ministry and purpose. It gives us some insight into what they are like, what they do, and who they minister to.

1. Ministering spirits

Angels are spiritual beings, which means we cannot see them unless God opens our eyes to the spirit realm. Therefore, many of their activities are unseen and may go unnoticed by humans. They are sent to minister, helping, assisting, and guiding people.

2. Sent by God to serve God

Angels do not act on their authority. God sends them to do His will and carry out specific tasks to serve Him.

3. For those who are to inherit salvation

Angels minister to believers who will inherit salvation through Christ. They protect, guide, and assist Christians in their spiritual journey. Did you notice how it says they minister to believers who will inherit salvation? In some cases, it may be in the future tense. I have already shared a story of when I believed angels watched over my life before I committed to Christ.

Max Lucado, Author and Pastor, says, "God's angels are here to minister to us in ways we do not see. They serve as His messengers and do the work of His will in our Lives."

John Piper, Theologian, says, "Angels are the sent ones, messengers and ministering spirits, bringing God's care to His people. They do not act on their own but are commissioned for God's purposes."

In the second century, a young man named Justin from Asia Minor studied various schools of Greek philosophy. One day, he was walking along a beach at Ephesus, pondering, as young people often do, about the meaning of life in general and his own life in particular, when a mysterious old man joined him in conversation. As they walked together, the old man spoke about philosophers and how none could answer life's most profound mysteries. He advised Justin to read the Old Testament prophets before disappearing into the distance. Justin became a Christian, one of the church's most significant early theologians, and one of its earliest martyrs for the faith – hence the name by which he is remembered today: Justin Martyr.

Angels may appear in dreams

I have heard people recount encounters with angels in their dreams. There are several biblical references to angels appearing in dreams.

Jacob - One of the most quoted is that of Jacob and his dream of a ladder on earth extending up to heaven with angels ascending and descending.

"Then he dreamed and behold, a ladder was set up on earth, and its top reached to heaven; and there the angels of God were ascending and descending on it." And behold, the Lord stood above it." Genesis 28:12-13. This is like a portal for angels between heaven and earth.

Joseph - In the New Testament, we read of an angel appearing to Joseph in a dream on multiple occasions.

"Behold, an angel of the Lord appeared to him in a dream, saying, "Joseph, son of David, do not be afraid to take you, Mary, your wife, for that which is conceived in her is of the Holy Spirit." Matthew 1:20-21.

Joseph needed assurance that Mary had conceived by the Holy Spirit.

Again, an angel appeared in a dream, telling Joseph they needed to flee to Egypt because King Herod would seek to destroy the child.

"Now when they had departed, behold, an angel of the Lord appeared to Joseph in a dream, saying, 'Arise, take the young child and his mother, flee to Egypt, and stay there until I bring you word, for Herod will seek the young child to destroy Him." Matthew 2:13.

After Herod's death, an angel appeared to Joseph again, instructing him to return to Israel.

"Now when Herod was dead, behold, an angel appeared in a dream to Joseph in Egypt, saying, 'Arise take the young Child and His mother, and go to the land of Israel, for those who sought the young Child's life are dead." Matthew 2:19-20.

Can animals at times see angels?

Is it possible for animals to sometimes see angels when we do not? The story of Balaam's donkey would indicate this is a possibility.

Balaam was persuaded by some people sent by Balak to come and curse the Israelites, but the Lord had told him not to go. However, he went, and an angel stood in their way.

"Then God's anger was aroused because he went, and the angel of the Lord took His stand in the way as an adversary against Him. And he was riding on his donkey, and his two servants were with him. Now the Donkey saw the angel of the Lord standing in the way with His drawn sword in His hand, and the donkey turned aside out of the way

and went into the field. So, Balaam struck the donkey to turn her back onto the road." Numbers 22:22-23.

This happened several times. *"Then the Lord opened the mouth of the donkey, and she said to Balaam, "What have I done to you, that you have struck me these three times?"* (Have you ever wondered what an animal might say to you if it could speak?).

Finally, we read. *"The Lord opened Balaam's eyes, and he saw the angel of the Lord standing in his way with His drawn sword in His hand, and he bowed his head and fell flat on his face."* Numbers 22:22-31.

The point is that animals may sometimes see angels in the spirit realm when we do not.

Angels ministering to Jesus

After Jesus had fasted for forty days and nights in the wilderness, He resisted and overcame the devil's temptations.

"Then the devil left Him, and behold, angels came and ministered to Him." Matthew 4:11.

The Gospel of Mark does not elaborate on the temptations as Matthew does, but adds to them. *"He was there in the wilderness forty days, tempted by Satan, and was with the wild beasts; and the angels ministered to Him."* Mark 1:13.

What kind of wild beasts were around in those days? Asiatic lions (but probably rare by then), leopards, wolves, hyenas, wild boars, jackals, serpents and scorpions. So, the implication is that angels would have protected Him.

When Jesus prayed in the Garden of Gethsemane, angels came and ministered to Him.

"Then an angel appeared to Him from heaven, strengthening Him. And being in agony, He prayed more earnestly. Then His sweat became like great drops of blood falling down to the ground." Luke 22:43-44

Angels were also seen at the time of His resurrection and Ascension. Matthew 28:2-7, Acts 1:10-11.

Angels ministering to the Apostles

In the book of Acts, there are several references to angels ministering to the Apostles.

"Then the high priest rose up, and all those who were with him (which is the sect of the Sadducees), and they were filled with indignation and laid hands on the Apostles and put them in the common prison. But at night. An angel of the Lord opened the prison doors, and brought them out, and said, "Go, stand in the temple and speak to the people all the words of this life." Acts 5:17-20.

Peter – He was in prison, but the church offered constant prayer to God on his behalf. God sent an angel to free Peter from prison.

"Behold, an angel of the Lord stood by him, and a light shone in the prison; and he struck Peter on the side and raised him up, saying, "Arise quickly!" and his chains fell off his hands" Acts12:5-8. Then the angel led him out of the prison.

Paul - All those in the boat with Paul are saved from a violent storm and shipwreck because of an angel that had appeared to Paul in the night.

"For there stood by me this night an angel of the God to whom I belong and whom I serve, saying, "Do not be afraid, Paul; you must be brought before Caesar; and indeed, God has granted you and all those who sail with you." Acts 27:23-24.

An angel directed Philip the evangelist

An angel directed Philip to go down a road through the desert from Jerusalem to Gaza.

"Now an angel of the Lord spoke to Philip, saying, "Arise and go toward the South along the road which goes down from Jerusalem to Gaza." Acts 8:26.

When he arrived, he was directed by the Spirit to join an Ethiopian man riding in a chariot. He heard him reading from the book of Isaiah and said, *"Do you understand what you are reading?"* he said, *"How can I unless someone guides me?" And he asked Philip to come and sit with him."* Philip explained that it spoke of the Messiah and that he preached Christ and the gospel to him. They stopped by some water, and Philip baptised him.

Angels and believers' deathbed stories

We also need to understand that angels will be present to minister to believers at the time of death. It would seem that our spirit may be escorted by angels into heaven.

The story of the rich man and Lazarus, the beggar, would suggest this possibility.

"So it was that the beggar died; and was carried by the angels to Abraham's bosom." Luke 16: 22.

I will share a few believers' deathbed stories that mention the waiting angels, presumably to escort them to heaven.

John G. Paton - His father had been a missionary, and he tells the story of his father's passing. As he neared death, his father suddenly opened his eyes wide and smiled. He then spoke softly, saying he could see a group of angels waiting for him. He described the beauty of their presence and the peace he felt before taking his last breath.

A Hospice Nurse – She tells the story of an elderly woman named Margaret who had been unconscious for hours. Suddenly, she opened her eyes and whispered joyfully, "They are here!" The angels have come for me." Her face lit up with joy as if she were seeing something indescribably beautiful. Moments later, she peacefully passed away.

Betty Eadie's experience – Betty underwent surgery in 1973 and was declared clinically dead for a short period. She was taken to a place of immense light and love, where she met angelic beings and Jesus. She felt an overwhelming sense of peace and was given insights into the purpose of life before being told she had to return to her body.

She later wrote Embraced by the Light, which became a well-known account of an NDE.

It is terrific that believers can look forward to seeing angels when they pass away and experience a peaceful transition from this earth to heaven.

Meeting loved ones in heaven

When David's son died, he said, *"Can I bring him back again? I shall go to him, but he shall not return to me."* 2 Samuel 12:23.

We will go to be with our loved ones who have already died and gone to heaven. This is something that all Christians eagerly anticipate.

Although there appears to be no direct reference to angels introducing us to loved ones in heaven, some scriptures indicate this possibility.

As mentioned in Luke 16:22, when the beggar died, angels carried him to *"Abraham's bosom."* This expression was something that the Jews understood as being taken to a place of comfort and peace when they died. This would have included being reunited with loved ones.

"And I say to you that many will come from the east and the west, and sit down with Abraham, Isaac, and Jacob in the kingdom of heaven." Matthew 8:11

We conclude that there will be times in heaven where we are not only in the presence of loved ones but also of the saints we have read about in the bible and history, as well as multitudes of angels.

"But you have come to Mount Zion and to the city of the living

God, the heavenly Jerusalem, to an innumerable company of angels, to the general assembly and church of the firstborn who are registered in heaven." Hebrews 12 22-23.

Chapter 6
Assisting God in answering prayer

"Peter was, therefore, kept in prison, but constant prayer was offered to God for him by the church..."Now behold, an angel of the Lord stood by him, and a light shone in the prison, and he struck Peter on the side and raised him up, saying, "Arise quickly!" And his chains fell off."

Acts 12:5-7.

The church offered constant prayer to God for Peter, who had been imprisoned. God responded by sending an angel to free him. Peter saw the angel, but how often do unseen angels assist God in answering our prayers, and we are unaware of it?

The church should never underestimate the power of corporate prayer. The early church was committed to prayer and emphasised corporate prayer as a regular part of church life.

"And they continued steadfastly in the apostles' doctrine and fellowship, in the breaking of bread, and in prayers." Acts 2:42.

We have already provided some references that verify the assistance of angels in answering prayer, but it is worth expounding on this topic in more detail.

However, let us be clear that we are not praying directly to angels or to Mary. We pray to our heavenly Father in the name of Jesus, the name above every other name, for an answer to our prayers. God will sometimes answer by using angels.

D. L. Moody, the Evangelist, says, "I have often seen in my own life how the Lord sends angels to aid in answering the prayers of His people. They work behind the scenes, bringing God's will to fruition in ways we may never see but can feel."

Billy Graham, the Evangelist, says, "God uses angels to carry out His will, and sometimes angels may intervene in our lives in ways we don't fully understand. They may deliver messengers or even bring about answers to our prayers."

Corrie ten Boom, Holocaust Survivor and Christian Author, says, "When I prayed for God's help, I often felt the comforting presence of angels, guiding me, reminding me that God's timing is perfect, and He is always near."

A Centurion of the Italian Regiment

Cornelius was devout; he feared God with his whole household, generously gave alms to the people, and prayed to God.

"About the ninth hour of the day, he saw clearly in a vision an angel of God coming in and saying to him, "Cornelius!" And when he observed him, he was afraid and said, "What is it, Lord?" So, he said to him, "Your prayers and your alms have come up for a memorial before God. "Now send men to Joppa, and send for Simon whose surname is Peter." Acts 10:15.

We see an interesting thought here in this scripture: *"Your prayers and alms have come up for a memorial before God."* I wonder if our prayers and giving of alms are recorded in heaven as a memorial.

Because Cornelius was a devout man who prayed, an angel was sent to him to find Peter to come and preach the gospel to him and his household. Peter eventually came and preached the gospel after God gave him a vision that the Gentiles were not unclean. While Peter was preaching, God poured out His Holy Spirit upon the Gentiles.

"While Peter was still speaking these words, the Holy Spirit fell on all those who heard the word."… "For they heard them speak with tongues and magnify God." Then Peter answered, "Can anyone forbid water, that these should not be baptised who have received the Holy Spirit just as we have?" And he commanded them to be baptised in the name of the Lord Jesus." Acts 10:44-48. This was a revival amongst the Gentiles.

Daniel was known as a man of prayer

An Angel in the lion's den with Daniel -

In the Old Testament, numerous references are made to angels assisting God in answering prayers. Daniel was known as a man of prayer, and on several occasions, God sent an angel to answer his prayers. I will share some of these instances.

Daniel faced a dilemma. When Darius became king, a decree was enforced. *"Whoever petitions any god or man for thirty days, except you, O king, shall be cast into the den of lions."* Daniel 6:7.

Daniel knew the king had signed the decree, but continued to pray. "Daniel knew that the writing was signed, he went home and in his upper room, with his windows open toward Jerusalem, he knelt down on his knees three times that day, and prayed and gave thanks before his God, as was his custom since early days. Daniel 6:10.

However, this was a trap; some officials sought to eliminate Daniel and reported the violation to the king.

The king respected Daniel and his belief, but he had no choice but to honour his decree, and reluctantly had Daniel thrown into the lion's den.

But the king told him, *"Your God whom you serve continually, He will deliver you."* Verse 16.

The king fasted that night and had a restless sleep. He was anxious to see what had happened to Daniel, so he went early in the morning to the lion's den and said,

"Daniel, servant of the living God, has your God, whom you serve continually, been able to deliver you from the lions?" Then Daniel said to the king, "O king, live forever! My God has sent his angel and shut the lion's mouths so that they have not hurt me because I was found innocent before Him; and also, O king, I have done no wrong before you." Daniel 6:20-22.

The Lord sent an angel because Daniel was a man of prayer. As a result, those who accused Daniel of betraying the king were thrown into the lion's den and torn apart.

An angel explains a prophecy to Daniel -

Daniel read Jeremiah's prophecy about the seventy-year exile and prayed for God's mercy on Israel. As he sought God in prayer, interceding for the people's sins, God sent the angel Gabriel to Daniel to explain the prophecy and vision to him.

"Yes, while I was speaking in prayer, the man Gabriel, whom I had seen in a vision at the beginning, being caused to fly swiftly, reached me about the time of the evening offering and informed me and talked with me, and said, "O Daniel I have now come forth to give you skill to understand. At the beginning of your supplications, the command went out, and I have come to tell you, for you are greatly beloved; therefore, consider the matter, and understand the vision." Daniel 9:21-23.

While he was praying, the command went out. From where? We can only assume it was from the throne of God. The angel Gabriel was dispatched to explain the vision to him.

An angel brings an answer to Daniel -

Daniel prayed and fasted for three weeks by the Tigris River. He has a heavenly vision of a glorious being (possibly Jesus or an angel) and is told about a spiritual battle in the unseen heavenly realm.

"Do not fear, Daniel, from the first day that you set your heart to understand and humble yourself before your God, your words were heard, and I have come because of your words. But the prince of the kingdom of Persia withstood me twenty-one days; and behold, Michael, one of the chief princes, came to help me, for I had been left alone there with the kings of Persia. Now I have come to tell you what will happen to your people in the latter days, for the vision refers to many days yet to come." Daniel 10:12-14. The vision is prophetic of what will happen in the last days concerning the kingdoms of the world and the kingdom of God.

An angel brings healing in answer to prayer -

This is an unusual testimony of an angel bringing healing. I cannot validate this, but it was published through Holy Spirit TV. When *Oretha Hagin* (the wife of *Kenneth Hagin*) was in her 70's the doctors diagnosed her with an incurable heart condition. She did not say, "Well, I am a Christian and live with a mighty man of God. I've listened to many sermons. Instead, she began to spend time in the word herself. She prayed and was led to listen to healing scripture tapes, playing them all night and all day wherever she was. She meditated on those scriptures for months. She refused to succumb to negativity and continued to listen to God's word. After a year of hearing the word, she was at home watching TV with her husband when she saw an angel enter the room. He stood before her, reached into her chest, and deposited something he was carrying. It was a new heart.

They went to the doctor shortly after. They didn't tell him anything that had happened. The doctor looked at it and said, "This isn't the same heart; it's a completely different organ." This is the first verified miracle I've ever personally witnessed because I'm telling you, this is a picture of a completely different heart.

This is unusual, for there are very few references to angels being used in some way to bring healing to people. But we must remember that all things are possible with God. The only other direct reference I am aware of to an angel being involved with healing people is in John 5:4, where an angel at certain times stirred the waters of the pool of Bethesda and the first person to step in was healed.

"A great multitude of sick people, blind, lame, paralysed, waiting for the moving of the water: For an angel went down at a certain time into the pool and stirred up the water; then whoever stepped in first, after the stirring of the water, was made well of whatever disease they had." (John 5:4).

Missionary to the New Hebrides

John G. Paton, a missionary to the New Hebrides, recounted that one particular night, hostile natives surrounded his home, intending to kill him. He and his wife prayed fervently. In the morning, the attackers had vanished. Later, a tribal chief told him they had seen large men in shining garments surrounding the house, which made them flee.

Angels on Assignment

In his book *Angels on Assignment*, Pastor Roland Buck shares multiple experiences of angelic visitations, often in response to profound prayer. He claimed the angels brought him messages, warnings, and divine protection.

Chapter 7

The fall of Satan and his angels

"And war broke out in heaven: Michael and his angels fought with the dragon, and the dragon and his angels fought, but they did not prevail, nor was there a place found in heaven any longer. So, the great dragon was cast out, that serpent of old; called the Devil and Satan, who deceives the whole world; was cast to the earth, and his angels were cast out with him."

Revelation 12:7-9.

We see in this scripture several names given to Satan. He is called the Great Dragon, the Serpent of Old, and the Devil. Some scholars believe that his angels are now regarded as demons.

Many other names and phrases in the Bible refer to Satan, such as; Lucifer, the ruler of this world, the prince of the power of the air, the evil one, the father of lies, Beelzebub (lord of the flies), Abaddon (destruction), Apollyon (destroyer), (angel of the bottomless pit), and possibly Leviathan.

Lucifer (Satan)

Lucifer seems to be the name that Satan held before his fall. It means "brightness" in Hebrew or "morning star."

"How are you fallen from heaven, O Lucifer, son of the morning! How are you cut down to the ground, you who weakened the nations!"

The answer is obvious: the following verses, reveal his pride and rebellion against God. He tried to take over from God. What we would call such a rebellion today is a coup d'état. The root is pride, which has been the cause of the rise and fall of many dictators.

"You said in your heart: I will ascend into heaven, I will extol my throne above the stars of God; I will also sit on the mount of the congregation, on the farthest sides of the north; I will ascend above the heights of the clouds, I will be like the Most-High. Yet you shall be brought down to Sheol, to the lowest depths of the Pit." Isaiah 14:12-15.

Augustine of Hippo says, "The devil, who was once an angel, became a devil by his own pride." Spot on, Augustine! Arrogance and pride are a seedbed for all kinds of dictatorial problems.

John Stott, in The Cross of Christ, says, "Satan, the deceiver of mankind, is a fallen angel, whose rebellion against God has become the origin of all evil in the world."

Lucifer, the anointed Cherub, before his fall

Lucifer would have been a leading light among the heavenly host before his fall. This is alluded to in Ezekiel. Although it mentions the king of Tyre, it also describes Lucifer as the anointed cherub.

"You were the seal of perfection, full of wisdom and perfect in beauty. You were in Eden, the garden of God; every precious stone was your covering: The sardius, topaz, diamond, beryl, onyx, jasper, sapphire, turquoise, and emerald with gold. The workmanship of your timbrels and pipes was prepared for you on the day you were created."

"You were the anointed cherub who covers; I established you; you were on the holy mountain of God; you walked back and forth in the midst of fiery stones. You were perfect in your ways until iniquity was found in you....Therefore, I cast you as a profane thing out of the mountain of God; and destroyed you, O covering cherub, from the midst of the fiery stones. Your heart was lifted up because of your beauty; you corrupted your wisdom for the sake of your splendour; I cast you to the ground." Ezekiel 28:12-17. There is speculation from v13 that he may have played music or even led worship in heaven. No wonder there is often contention in churches regarding worship and worship leaders.

Additionally, Tolkien, in his mythological work, The Silmarillion, includes an allegorical figure of Melkor, who is often associated with the figure of Satan. When Illuvatar (God) plays a song of creation, Melkor joins in but then plays his own discordant tune. Illuvatar changes the melody a few times, and Melkor keeps subverting the music, but rather than stop it altogether, Illuvatar keeps playing, knowing that something even more beautiful will arise at the end. It makes you wonder if Tolkien borrowed from passages like this in his mythology?

He would have held a high position among the heavenly hosts as the anointed cherub. He would have been an influential and radiant figure, in all his beauty, wisdom, and power, who could easily attract a following before iniquity was found in him. Despite his beauty, he was cast out as profane, which led to his pride and downfall.

Jesus saw Satan fall from heaven

In His eternal state before his human form, Jesus witnessed the fall of Satan and his angels. The disciples came to Jesus, overjoyed because demons were subject to them in His name.

"And He said to them, "I saw Satan fall like lightning from heaven. Behold, I give you authority to trample on serpents and scorpions, and over all the power of the enemy, and nothing shall by any means hurt you. Nevertheless, do not rejoice in this, that the spirits are subject to you, but rather rejoice because your names are written in heaven." Luke 10: 17-20.

Yes, we have authority over evil spirits in Jesus' name, but the important thing is that our names are eternally recorded in heaven by becoming believers and followers of Christ.

This raises another question about whether fallen angels and demons are the same. Christian leaders have different views. This has become a debatable subject; we will endeavour to explore it.

Fallen angels and demons

Many Christian leaders and theologians teach that demons

are fallen angels who rebelled with Satan (Rev 12:4) on the premise that both oppose God and afflict people (Matthew 12:24-26).

Others believe that fallen angels and demons are distinct. This suggests that fallen angels are powerful spiritual beings with spiritual bodies, while demons are disembodied spirits seeking to possess a body. (Luke 8:30-31).

We are not told a lot about the fallen angels except that they are no longer in heaven but have been cast down to hell, restricted by chains, and awaiting their final judgment. This could be in the future, as they are still able to help Satan carry out his evil work.

"For if God did not spare the angels who sinned, but cast them down to hell and delivered them into chains of darkness, to be reserved for judgment." 2 Peter 2:4.

"And the angels who did not keep their proper domain, but left their own abode, He has reserved in everlasting chains under darkness for the judgment of the great day." Jude 6.

Both scriptures are written in the context that no one who has sinned without repenting and knowing Christ will escape the judgment to come.

In case you are wondering, the fallen angels and demons who have sinned and rebelled against God will never be offered redemption; their final destination will be confined to hell.

The word reserved may be the key, meaning they are still active today under Satan but awaiting their final judgment.

Satan has a hierarchy that includes the use of fallen angels because we read in Ephesians that Christians battle against spiritual forces.

"Put on the whole armour of God, that you may be able to stand against the wiles of the devil. For we do not wrestle against flesh and blood, but against principalities, against powers, against the rulers of the darkness of this age, against spiritual hosts of wickedness in the heavenly places." Ephesians 6: 11-12.

As noted, some scholars believe this hierarchy is composed of fallen angels, including lower-ranked ones that act as demons or disembodied spirits that wander, seeking to possess bodies. "When an unclean spirit goes out of a man, he goes through dry places, seeking rest; and finding none, he says, *"I will return to my house from which I came."* Luke 11:24-26.

Do fallen angels masquerade as aliens?

I am inclined to think that many of the hardcore alien abductions are encounters with demonic forces pretending to be aliens. Some Christians have conducted research into this subject. However, most people caught up in this phenomenon prefer to think of these beings as "enlightened."

But if these beings are so enlightened, why do they do such horrible things in secret, and why do they struggle when asked about Jesus?

This also makes me think that some clairvoyants and spiritists may not be connecting with deceased relatives, but rather with demonic familiar spirits that are aware of their loved ones' past.

TV shows and movies have popularised the subject of angels in various ways, although they have captivated people's minds across cultures for generations.

The reality of spiritual warfare

When I served as an assistant pastor in my twenties, the senior pastor's wife, *Jillene Oxley*, a faithful prayer warrior, led a prayer warfare meeting. I was asked to co-lead with her. We spent much time in prayer, resisting the powers of darkness that dominate the nations, especially in Australia. I was a little sceptical of its effectiveness until I had a dream.

In this dream, I was the personal bodyguard for the Prime Minister of Australia. I lived in a bungalow at the back of the Prime Minister's residence. I heard a noise, looked out the window, and saw a fleet of black objects flying in formation. Two black objects spotted me and broke formation as I looked, heading straight for me. Sensing they were evil, I grabbed my revolver and started shooting at them, but it had no effect; they came in the window and attacked me. At that moment, the dream became a reality; I started choking as there was pressure on my neck and chest. (My wife thought I was having a heart attack.) But I managed to whisper the name "JESUS," and the black objects fled in terror. I woke up and tried to explain to my wife what had happened.

I asked the Lord what that was all about, desperate to understand what had just happened and why. I started praying and searching the scriptures for an answer until I found one.

"For though we walk in the flesh, we do not war in the flesh. For the weapons of our warfare are not carnal but mighty in God for pulling down strongholds, casting down arguments and every high thing that exalts itself against the knowledge of God, bringing every thought into captivity to the obedience of Christ." 2 Corinthians 10:3-5.

I believe God revealed to me the reality of spiritual warfare through this experience. Carnal weapons were of no effect. But we have mighty weapons in God, the Name of Jesus, the Word of God, the power of the Holy Spirit, our faith in who we are in Christ, and our authority in Him. We are engaged in a spiritual battle, as mentioned in Ephesians 6:10-20.

An angelic encounter in warfare

I will never forget that, on one occasion during one of the meetings I have described above, we broke through in the Spirit. We were very conscious of the presence of God, and we all ended up prostrate with our faces to the floor. There was a holy hush, and at that moment, I saw in my mind's eye (I'm not sure how to describe it) an angel engulfed in a brilliant golden glow standing over us with his sword in hand, pointing it down toward his feet, signifying that the battle had been won. As I watched in awe, I saw another angel fly by, tap him on the shoulder, and say, "Come, we have more battles to win."

The people left the prayer meeting individually, but I

remained for another hour. During this time, I felt sad and began to weep. I did not understand what was happening, so I asked the Lord.

He replied, "You feel what I feel when I am rejected, even though the battle has been won." I felt He was referring to the cross and the Lord's death, burial, and resurrection. The Lord said, "What more could I do than I have already done?" I did not fully understand until I later read,

"What more could have been done to My vineyard that I have not done in it? Why then, when I expect to bring forth good grapes, did I bring forth wild grapes?" Isaiah 5:4.

In its context, it possibly refers to the way Israel and the Jews have rejected Jesus. Although I felt the Lord was showing me that when it comes to salvation, the proclamation of the gospel, the formation of the church, and the kingdom of God, God can do no more; it is now up to the church to act.

If God feels what He has done is sometimes rejected, be encouraged when we also think that way. Let us continue to proclaim the gospel, regardless of the outcome.

Demonic forces appear to be territorial

The Bible would indicate that they are territorial. Daniel prayed from the first day, and his prayers were heard, but a spiritual battle raged in the heavens before the answer came.

"But the prince of the kingdom of Persia withstood me twenty-one days, and behold, Michael, one of the chief princes, came to help me, for

I had been left alone with the king of Persia."…. "Now, I must return and fight with the prince of Persia." Daniel 10:13, 20.

When Jesus was confronted with a demon-possessed man in the territory of the Gadarenes, the demons, sensing they were about to be cast out, begged to stay in the region.

"Then He asked him, "What is your name?" And he answered, saying, "My name is legion, for we are many." Also, he begged Him earnestly that He would not send them out of the country." Mark 5:9-10.

A young missionary in the highlands of Papua New Guinea (PNG) told me they had been struggling to achieve a breakthrough in their area for several years. One night, he woke up to find a demon standing at the foot of his bed, looking like an old man with dreadlocks. The demon told him, "You must leave this area. The people here have belonged to me for centuries; they are mine, not yours. The missionary said, "No, you're wrong." They have been redeemed by the blood of Jesus, who came to set them free. Now I command you, in the name of Jesus, to leave this area." Not long after, a revival broke out in the area.

Therefore, demonic forces could have extensive networks spanning multiple nations, regions, cities, towns, villages, influential individuals, and leaders, including those in the armed forces and political parties. I would also suggest some organisations.

The work of demons

Demons are also referred to as evil spirits and devils; they appear to have specific names, as Jesus named several: a spirit of infirmity, an unclean spirit, a deaf and dumb spirit, and a legion or many spirits.

Demons take control of areas of a person's body; this may influence the person's actions and speech, and they may become tormented mentally or physically and are often violent. They are evil in every respect and are intent on destroying us and keeping us from responding to the gospel.

They are also masters at spreading lies and deceiving people, even infiltrating the church with false doctrine and *"doctrines of demons"* (1 Timothy 4:1). While writing this, a small extremist group of Christians in Australia, including the pastor, family members and others have been found guilty of the manslaughter of an eight-year-old diabetic girl who died because they refused to give her prescribed insulin. They believed God would heal her. Yes, God can heal directly in answer to prayer, but He often uses the medical profession to bring healing. We need faith and wisdom when it comes to divine healing today.

How can we deal with demons today?

Jesus set the example by demonstrating His authority over demons, casting them out. We can learn to do the same. "And they were astonished at His teaching, for He taught them as one having authority, and not as the scribes. Now, there was a man in their synagogue with an unclean spirit. And cried out, saying, *"Leave us alone! What have we to do with you, Jesus of Nazareth? Did you come to destroy us? I know who you are - the Holy*

One of God!" But Jesus rebuked him, saying, "Be quiet and come out of him!" And when the unclean spirit convulsed him and cried out with a loud voice, he came out of him." Mark 1:22-26.

The above scripture is interesting as it provides insight into a few aspects of demons, which I will describe.

- It is an unclean spirit (unholy)
- It wants to be left alone (to do its work)
- It knows Jesus can destroy it (fears Jesus)
- It recognises Jesus as the Holy Son of God
- It had to obey Jesus and come out

To summarise the above, demons do not want to be discovered or disturbed; it demonstrates how they want to be left alone to complete their destructive work, which includes trying to keep people from turning to Christ.

This subject raises the question, "Can a demon possess a believer?" There are two schools of thought. Yes and no. It is a controversial issue. Most traditional churches would say the believer is filled with the Holy Spirit and can only be influenced or attacked by demons.

However, we must recognise that Jesus has given believers the power and authority to cast out demons.

"And these signs shall follow those who believe: in My name, they shall cast out demons; they shall speak with new tongues; they shall take up serpents; and if they drink anything deadly, it will by no means hurt them; they will lay hands on the sick, and they will recover." Mark 16:17-18.

The apostles cast out demons in Jesus' name. There is the example of Paul's encounter with a slave girl.

"A certain slave girl possessed with a spirit of divination met us, who brought her masters much profit by fortune telling. This girl followed Paul and us crying out, saying, "These men are servants of the Most-High God, who proclaim to us the way of salvation." And this she did for many days, but Paul, greatly annoyed, turned and said to the spirit, "I command you in the name of Jesus Christ to come out of her." And he came out that very hour." Acts 16:16-18.

The above scripture reveals the deceptive nature of demons. What she was saying was true. But she overdid it, and Paul knew in his spirit that it was a spirit of divination. Religious spirits can behave similarly.

Personal encounters with demons

I have encountered demons in Australia, but mainly on the mission field in Papua New Guinea (they are deeply entrenched in their cultural background).

One of my first encounters was when I was preaching in a public hall one night in a small town in Victoria. Several people came forward when I gave an altar call. Suddenly, one of the women who came forward put her hands over her ears and started screaming, "I hate your preaching." Sensing it was a demon, I demanded to know why! In a loud guttural voice, she cried, "Too much truth, I hate the truth." I commanded the demon to come out of her.

Then, in the same tone of voice and in a mocking way,

she started screaming, "No, no, no, because help is on the way." She started screaming again and again. Then, someone started knocking on the door we had closed because of the noise she was making. They were saying, "What's going on in there?" Open the door."

We were reluctant to open the door, but thought it might have been the police. To our surprise, it was two people from a well-known sect in the area. Unfortunately, we had to call it a night.

Keys to dealing with demons

- Know who you are in Christ
- Know your authority in Christ
- Know the power of the blood of Christ
- Know the power of the name of Jesus
- Know the power of His word
- Know how to resist the devil
- Know how to command them to come out

What do we hope to accomplish?

Some people are sceptical and wonder if spiritual warfare and deliverance through prayer will make any difference.

The Bible indicates that it will make a difference, and besides, Jesus cast out demons, as did the apostles. The epistles inform us that we are engaged in a spiritual battle and possess the authority to participate in spiritual warfare. The anointing of the Holy Spirit will enable us to break bondages.

- It will fend off enemy attacks.
- It will advance the kingdom of God.
- It will strengthen our faith.
- It will bring freedom and liberty.
- It will glorify God.

DO ANGELS WALK AMONG US TODAY?

Chapter 8

Angels desire to look into the gospel

"To them, it was revealed that; not to themselves, but to us they were ministering the things, which now have been reported to you through those who have preached the gospel to you by the Holy Spirit sent from heaven - things which angels desire to look into."

1 Peter 1:12

What does the above scripture mean? It reveals that Angels find the gospel somewhat of a mystery. It says, "they desire to look into it, a phrase in the Greek, implying a longing to peer into, or investigate, just like someone bends down to examine something more closely.

Angels are magnificent beings and highly intelligent, but not omniscient like God. It implies they are still learning and understanding how God deals with humanity.

Angels have known only holiness and do not require forgiveness or salvation. They marvel at the gospel of God's grace, seeking to understand why God would offer such a wonderful redemption to unholy sinners.

Angels are in awe of our salvation; they have not sinned and are therefore unaware of the guilt and shame that humans experience. As spiritual beings, they have not succumbed to the vile temptations of the flesh and fallen into sin as we have. They must wonder at our lack of holiness and purity.

Tim Keller, Theologian and Author, says, "Angels are witnesses to the gospel, but not its messengers. The message of the gospel is entrusted to humans, not because they are more capable but because they are the ones who experience the grace of God in a fallen world. The gospel is personal to us in a way it cannot be to angels."

Angels do not qualify to preach the gospel

So, angels do not qualify to preach the gospel of grace as we do. They are amazed at God's love, wisdom, power and plan of redemption.

Angels do not get to preach the gospel; that privilege is reserved for humans who have experienced God's saving grace through our Lord Jesus Christ. Angels often deliver messages and protect and direct believers, but they are not flesh-and-blood beings who have had to struggle with our sinful nature. They cannot be evangelists who understand redemption.

Find Peter to come and preach the gospel

An angel appeared to Cornelius with a message and gave him instructions to find the apostle Peter, so that Peter could come and preach the gospel. However, the angel did not preach the gospel to him.

"And when he observed him (an angel), he was afraid and said, "What is it, lord?" So, he said to him, "Your prayers and your alms have come up for a memorial before God." "Now send men to Joppa, and send for Simon, a tanner, whose house is by the sea. He will tell you what you must do." Acts 10:4-5.

They went and found Peter, who reluctantly came with them back to Cornelius's household. Because they were Gentiles. Peter preached the gospel to them and had a fantastic response.

"While Peter was still speaking these words, the Holy Spirit fell on all those who heard the word. And those of the circumcision who believed were astonished, as many as came with Peter, because the gift of the Holy Spirit had been poured out on the Gentiles also. For they heard them speak with tongues and magnify God. Then Peter answered, "Can anyone forbid water, that these should not be baptised, who have received the Holy Spirit just as we have?" And he commanded them to be baptised in the name of the Lord. Then they asked him to stay a few days. Acts 10:44-48.

The angel did not preach the gospel; he only brought the message and gave direction for Cornelius to send for Peter to come and preach the gospel, resulting in an outpouring of the Holy Spirit.

The great commission was given to humans

Jesus commanded His disciples, not angels, to go into the world and preach the gospel.

"Jesus came and spoke to them (His disciples), saying, "All authority has been given to Me in heaven and on earth. Go therefore, and make disciples of all nations, baptising them in the name of the Father and of the Son and of the Holy Spirit, teaching them to observe all things that I have commanded you; and lo, I am with you always, even to the end of the age." Matthew 28: 16-20.

Angels are not commissioned to preach the gospel, make disciples, baptise, or teach people. It is given to the church, which comprises believers and ministers who are called to this tremendous responsibility. Jesus gave some disciples ministry gifts.

"And He Himself gave some to be apostles, some prophets, some evangelists, and some pastors and teachers, for the equipping of the saints for the work of ministry, for the edifying of the body of Christ." Ephesians 4:11-12.

God uses human weakness for His power

God displays His wisdom and power through human weakness. He uses redeemed humanity with all its imperfections and frailty to demonstrate His power to the world. This probably seems like a foolish plan to the angels who desire to look into and understand how redemption works.

When God calls us to minister, He knows we are imperfect

and will fail occasionally. However, it is His way of keeping us humble so we do not become proud and boast about our own glory. God chooses to reach the lost through human weakness.

"For you see your calling, brethren, that not many wise according to the flesh, not many mighty, not many noble, are called. But God has chosen the foolish things of the world to put to shame the wise, and God has chosen the weak things of the world to put to shame the things which are mighty; and the base things of the world and the things which are despised God has chosen, and the things which are not, to bring to nothing the things that are, that no flesh should glory in His presence. But of Him, you are in Christ Jesus, who became for us wisdom from God – and righteousness and sanctification and redemption – that as it is written, "He who glories, let Him glory in the Lord." 1 Corinthians 26-31.

When God called me into the ministry to become a pastor, I felt utterly inadequate until I read the above scripture. I did not see myself as gifted or talented. However, I had a heart to know and love God and a desire to serve Him and help people.

My wife and I were married and only had a short honeymoon before enrolling in a Bible College in another state to train for ministry. All we had was a carload of wedding presents. We stopped on the outskirts of Adelaide to buy a paper and look for somewhere to rent. We found a flat near the Bible college we would attend for the next two years. We worked during the day and attended the College every night.

After graduating from Bible college, we returned to Melbourne, where we worked during the day and pioneered a small church on weekends in Healesville. We hired an old scout hall and had about forty people after twelve months. I was then invited to join the full-time ministry team of a large charismatic church in Melbourne, where I served for six years before God called us to Papua New Guinea (PNG).

Angels observe humanity and the gospel

Angels observe imperfect humans preaching the gospel and fulfilling the great commission.

Angels saw the fall of Satan with his rebellious angels. They would have witnessed the fall of humanity and the sin and corruption of mankind.

Angels witnessed the birth of Christ and observed Jesus take on human flesh, suffer, and die on the cross for the sins of humanity.

Angels observed the transformation when sinners repented and turned to Christ.

Angels observe and celebrate each salvation.

"Likewise, I say to you, there is joy in the presence of the angels of God over one sinner who repents." Luke 15:10.

Angels are amazed at the love and grace of God and His redemptive plan of salvation.

Chapter 9

False angels can deceive us

"There are some who trouble you and want to pervert the gospel of Christ. But even if we, or an angel from heaven, preach any other gospel to you than what we have preached to you, let him be accursed."

Galatians 1:7-8.

We have already established that angels are not commissioned to preach the gospel. Paul warns the church that if even an angel from heaven preaches a gospel other than the one you have already received, you are being deceived.

A classic example is Joseph Smith, the founder of the Latter-day Saints, also known as the Mormons, who claimed that the angel Moroni appeared to him and gave him the Book of Mormon. Most Christians believe this was not an actual angel but either a deceiving spirit disguised as one or a lie from Joseph Smith, who had previously been taken to court on charges of fraud. He was accused of taking people's money to unsuccessfully locate hidden treasure through the use of magic seeing stones.

Deceiving spirits and doctrines of demons

We have been warned that in the last days, some will depart from the faith because of deceiving spirits and doctrines of demons.

"Now the Spirit expressly says that in latter times some will depart from the faith, giving heed to deceiving spirits and doctrines of demons." 1 Timothy 4:1.

The lyrics to a popular Elvis Presley song, *You're the Devil in Disguise*, portray how easy it is to be deceived by something that appears to be good.

You look like an angel (look like an angel)
Walk like an angel (walk like an angel)
Talk like an angel
But I got wise
You're the devil in disguise
Oh, yes, you are the devil in disguise.

The song is likely about a seductive and deceptive woman, but the point is that we need to be wise enough to discern the deception.

Helena Blavatsky, founder of the Theosophical Society, claimed to receive wisdom from "Ascended Masters," spirit beings who guided her to develop a new religious philosophy. Many believe these so-called "Masters" were deceptive spirits, as her teachings contradict Biblical Christianity and align more with Occultism and Eastern Mysticism.

Emmanuel Swedenborg, A Swedish Scientist and mystic, claimed to have visited heaven and hell and conversed with angels and spirits. His teaching departs from traditional Christian beliefs, denying the Trinity and introducing controversial doctrines.

A personal encounter with a deceptive woman

Our church in Lismore was in the heart of the city, and we often had people wander in off the street. As the senior pastor, I was in the front row of our morning service. I had my eyes closed and was enjoying a precious time of worship when I felt someone standing before me.

When I opened my eyes, I was startled to see a young lady standing before me, looking up into my eyes. She said, "Give me the microphone. I am the angel, Grace, from the Book of Revelation and have a message for the church. I couldn't think of an angel named Grace in the Book of Revelation.

So, I said, "No, you're not the angel, Grace, so go and sit down, and I will speak to you after the meeting. She went and sat down but left the meeting before it ended. I often wonder what she would have said, but I'm sure it would have been questionable.

Satanic angels of light

"For such are false prophets, deceitful workers. Transforming themselves into apostles of Christ. And no wonder! For Satan himself transforms

himself into an angel of light. Therefore, it is no great thing if his ministers also transform themselves into ministers of righteousness, whose end will be according to their works." 1 Corinthians 11:14-15.

If Satan can transform himself into an angel of light, so can his ministers (people he uses and fallen angels). Some people may appear genuine and seem to say all the right things, but we must discern whether it is God or a deception.

Over the years, I have observed false prophets making outlandish predictions and assigning dates to events, but when they do not come true, they are too proud to admit it.

We have been warned of deception in the end times. Jesus put it at the head of a list of signs to watch out for in the last days.

Take heed, no one deceives you

When the disciples of Jesus came and asked Him what the sign of His coming and the end of the age would be, He gave them more than one sign. He provided an extensive list, but began with what was probably the most important and obvious one.

"Take heed that no one deceives you. For many will come in My name, saying, "I am the Christ," and will deceive many….."Then many false prophets will rise up and deceive many" Matthew 24:4-5 and 11.

Take heed (beware, this is a warning) that no one deceives you or leads you astray. It could also refer to the moral decline in our society (V10-12). Many Christians today overlook the first thing Jesus mentioned (deception) and jump straight into trying to interpret all the signs beginning at verse 6, which concern the conflict and rumours of wars, a topic also relevant to us today.

However, deception should be our primary concern; it is already rife in the world we live in today. I elaborate on this in my last book, *"Seems Like a Good Idea."*

Paul warns young Timothy of the power of deception in the last days, which will cause people to depart from the faith.

"Now the Spirit expressly says that in the latter times, some will depart from the faith, giving heed to deceiving spirits and doctrines of demons, speaking lies in hypocrisy." 1 Timothy 4:1-2.

This is why we see so many cults, occult, and new-age teachings as an alternative to authentic Christianity.

In Papua New Guinea (PNG) and the Pacific Islands, there are several "Cargo Cults." They arose when indigenous people did not understand Western economies. They observed the supply of various goods associated with supernatural or ancestral forces and believed that by performing specific rituals, they could attract similar goods, or cargo. Many of these practices have emerged because of false angels and deceiving spirits that have created demonic doctrines.

When we were in PNG, we had a lovely expatriate family attending the church in Port Moresby. They decided to leave the church and join the Bahá'í Faith because they were drawn to the alternative lifestyle associated with the faith at the time.

The Baha'i Faith holds Jesus in high regard, recognising Him as a manifestation of God, similar to figures like Buddha, Krishna, and Muhammad.

The Bahá'í teachings are subtle; they teach that He is divinely inspired but not the literal Son of God – instead, He reflects the perfection of God. They do not believe in the Trinity and hold differing views on the atonement and the resurrection.

"For the time will come when they will not endure sound doctrine, but according to their own desires, because they have itching ears, they will heap-up for themselves teachers; and they will turn their ears away from the truth, and be turned aside by fables." 2 Timothy 4:3-4.

Lies about angelic visitations

Some Christians and prophets with a ministry may even lie about angelic visitations to appear spiritual.

A good example of this is found in 1 Kings 13. It's about a man of God and an old prophet. God sent a young man of God to prophesy against King Jeroboam's altar, which he had built at Bethel.

God had explicitly commanded him not to eat or drink in that place and to return another way. However, the old prophet from Bethel deceived him. He lied, claiming that an angel had spoken to him, telling him that the young man of God should return to his house and eat with him.

"Then he said to him, "Come home with me and eat bread." And he

said, "I cannot return with you or go in with you; neither can I eat bread or drink water with you in this place." "For I have been told by the word of the Lord. "You shall not eat bread or drink water there, nor return by the way you came." He said to him, "I too am a prophet as you are, and an angel spoke to me by the word of the Lord, saying, "Bring him back with you to your house, that he may eat bread and drink water." (He was lying to him.) So, he went back with him and ate bread in his house, and drank water." 1 Kings 13:15‑19.

While they were in the middle of fellowshipping, eating and drinking, the old prophet prophesied over the young man of God who came from Judah, saying,

"Thus says the Lord: Because you have disobeyed the word of the Lord, and have not kept the commandment which the Lord your God commanded you"….. "Your corpse shall not come to the tomb of your fathers." 1Kings 13:21-22.

The young man of God left on his donkey, but a lion met him on the road and killed him. Later, the old prophet appeared to be remorseful. He went and got the corpse and laid it in his tomb. As a result, what he prophesied came to pass. He also told his sons that when he died, they were to bury him on top of the man of God.

Like me, you are probably trying to work out the motive of the old prophet for doing this to the young man of God, as it appears to make little sense.

- Was he jealous, thinking he was to be replaced?
- Was he lonely and wanted to spend time with him?
- Was he trying to prove he was a better prophet?

- Was he testing him on behalf of God?
- Was he being used to bring judgment?

Whatever it was, it highlights the importance of the word of God and obedience to it. The old prophet had lied to him, telling him that an angel had instructed him to come home with him.

So, the young man of God was deceived into thinking that the word of an angel could override the word of the Lord—a big mistake.

This story cautions against trusting individuals who claim to have received divine revelation without verification from others or aligning it with the Word of God. This is how many weird sects and movements have commenced.

It also highlights our need for discernment to distinguish between right and wrong and the importance of obeying God's word.

Recorded encounters with false angels

Apart from modern-day incidents that, unfortunately, will continue to occur. There are several historical accounts recorded of people having encounters with false angels. We have already mentioned Joseph Smith. I will share a few more with you.

St. Padre Pio -

He was a renowned Italian mystic and priest frequently visited by supernatural beings. One night, he was approached by what appeared to be a radiant angel. However, he sensed something was off when he began interacting with it. Through prayer and testing the spirit, he discerned that it was a demon disguised as an angel of light. The false angel soon revealed its true nature and left in a rage.

St. Ignatius -

He developed a method for discerning spirits, outlined in his "Spiritual Exercises." He realised that evil spirits often appear good initially, but ultimately leave a person disturbed, anxious, or farther away from God. He once had an encounter with an angel, which he later discerned was not from God, as it led to pride rather than humility. His teachings emphasise testing the fruits of any spiritual experience.

A modern-day preacher (name withheld)

The preacher was intensely praying when he felt a presence offering him guidance. The entity claimed to be an angel from God and even quoted some scripture. He remembered 1 John 4:1, *"Beloved, do not believe every spirit, but test the spirits to see whether they are of God; because many false prophets have gone out into the world."* When he prayed in Jesus' name for the spirit to reveal its true nature, the presence vanished immediately, confirming it was a deceptive spirit.

Some guidelines for discerning false angels?

Test the spirits –

As we have just quoted in the previous paragraph, we are

instructed in 1 John 4:1 not to believe every spirit, but to test the spirits to see whether they are of God, because many false prophets have gone out into the world.

What is your gut feeling? What is your spirit telling you? Does it seem right? Is it based on the Bible? (1 John 2:20).

What is their attitude toward Jesus? -

The Incarnation of Christ is one sure way to test the spirits. Do they confess that Christ has come in the flesh?

"By this, you know the Spirit of God: every spirit that confesses that Jesus Christ has come in the flesh is of God, and every spirit that does not confess that Jesus Christ has come in the flesh is not of God, and this is the spirit of antichrist, which you have heard is coming and is now in the world." 1 John 4:2-3. An antichrist spirit may appear to be genuine but will ultimately be deceptive and will prove to be anti-Christian.

Test their message against scripture -

Does their message line up with the word of God? "But even if we, or an angel from heaven, preach any other gospel to you than what we have preached to you, let him be accursed." Galatians 1:8.

What is the fruit of their influence? -

It is usually the opposite of the fruit of the Spirit. False angels usually bear fruit of deception, lies, pride, fear, intimidation, accusation, and confusion.

Jesus said, *"Every good tree bears good fruit, but a bad tree bears bad fruit."….."Therefore, by their fruits you will know them."* Matthew 7:17 and 20.

Do they desire to be worshipped? -

They should never desire to be worshipped or glorified in any way. When John attempted to worship, an angel, the angel said, *"See that you do not do that!" "I am your fellow servant and of your brethren who have the testimony of Jesus. Worship God!"* Revelation 19:10.

Notice, however, that when the disciples worshipped the resurrected Jesus on two occasions, He did not rebuke them (Matthew 28:9, 17).

Check for occult connections -

True angels do not participate in seances, mystical rituals, or new-age mysticism. Deuteronomy 18:10-12 warns against divination, necromancy, and spiritism.

Pray for Discernment -

If something does not feel right, we should pray for wisdom and discernment, asking the Holy Spirit to reveal the truth.

DO ANGELS WALK AMONG US TODAY?

Chapter 10
Angels used in times of judgment

"And when the angel stretched out his hand over Jerusalem to destroy it, the Lord relented from the destruction; and said to the angel who was destroying the people. "It is enough; now restrain your hand."

2 Samuel 24:16

God uses angels to dispense His judgment and justice as a part of His divine order and authority. The Bible records many accounts of God dispatching angels throughout history to bring judgment on those who have sinned and rejected His grace and mercy.

We often get a false notion of angels from plays performed by Sunday school children. They are portrayed as cute, harmless, angelic beings with wings, flying around, ever ready to help and sustain us.

Angels are messengers who assist in salvation and watch

over believers in Christ, but they also serve as avengers who use their great power to fulfil God's will regarding His Judgments.

In the Middle Ages, many apocryphal and mystic texts record angels executing divine judgment, depicting angels as bringing plagues or disasters upon cities or nations as punishment for their sins.

In his *Systematic Theology*, Wayne Grudem, an American New Testament scholar and theologian, describes angels as both messengers and executors of God's decrees, including acts of judgment.

Grace in times of judgment

Despite some severe judgments in the Bible, God often displays grace in various ways to the righteous. (see examples below.) I have elaborated on God's amazing grace in relation to the gospel in my book, "But for the Grace of God Go I."

Noah and his family –

Although angels are not mentioned directly when God decided to destroy the world with a flood because of the wickedness of man, it grieved the heart of God that He had made man. But Noah and his family found grace in the eyes of the Lord.

"So, the Lord said, "I will destroy man whom I have created from the face of the earth, both man and beast, creeping thing and birds of the air, for I am sorry I have made them." But Noah found grace in the eyes of the Lord." Genesis 6:7-8

Lot and his family –

God shows grace to Lot and his family while they live in Sodom before He destroys the city. God sent two angels to visit Lot in Sodom to warn him of God's intention to destroy the city.

"When the morning dawned, the angels urged Lot to hurry, saying, "Arise, take your wife and your two daughters who are here, lest you be consumed in the punishment of the city." And while he lingered, the men took hold of his hand, and the hands of his two daughters, the Lord being merciful to him, and they brought him out and set him outside the city." Genesis 19:15-16.

Lot did not want to flee to the mountains, so he asked the angels to spare the nearby small city of Zoar. It was one of the five cities of the plain: Sodom, Gomorrah, Admah, Zeboiim, and Zoar (Genesis 14:1). The angels agreed, and as soon as Lot entered the city of Zoar, it rained down brimstone and fire from the Lord out of the heavens on Sodom and Gomorrah.

In his book *"All About Angels,"* C. Leslie Miller states, "It is significant that although Lot, Abraham's nephew, had drifted far from the holy standards of his uncle and had sought the companionship and material benefits of an unholy alliance, yet the angels of the Lord were there to spare his life and assist him in avoiding the consequences of his poor judgment."

Moses and Israel in Egypt -

God brings judgment on Egypt but shows grace to Israel. The Passover blood of the Lamb sprinkled upon the houses of the Israelites spared them from the destroying angel, bringing judgment on Pharaoh and Egypt by killing all the firstborns in the land.

"For the Lord will pass through to strike the Egyptians; and when he sees the blood on the lintel and on the doorposts, the Lord will pass over the door and not allow the destroyer to come into your house to strike you." Exodus 12:23.

King David and Israel -

King David sinned by taking a census of Israel when he was meant to trust in the Lord and His strength. The Lord was angry and sent an angel to bring a plague as judgment. As mentioned in the opening verse of scripture to this chapter, the angel was seen by David, who pleaded with God to stop.

"So, the Lord sent a plague upon Israel from the morning until the appointed time. From Dan to Beersheba, seventy thousand men of the people died. And when the angel stretched out his hand over Jerusalem to destroy it, the Lord relented from the destruction and said to the angel who was destroying the people, "It is enough, now restrain your hand.... Then David spoke to the Lord when he saw the angel who was striking the people, and said, "Surely I have sinned, and have done wickedly; but these sheep, what have they done?" "Let your hand, I pray, be against me and against my father's house." 2 Samuel 24:15-17.

I find this judgment to be harsh, but God was angry with David for taking the census for the following reasons -

- It demonstrated a lack of trust in God. By numbering the people, he put his trust in the strength of men, not God.

- God did not command it. There were conditions in the law for taking a census, which David did not adhere to (Exodus 30:12).

- Satan incited David to take the census. This caused David to act out of pride and self-reliance (1 Chronicles 21:1).

It is also interesting to note that Joab, David's military commander, objected to the census, indicating that he thought it was sinful. But David refused to heed his advice. "But why does my lord the king desire this thing?" (2 Samuel 24:3).

God's anger abated when David acknowledged his sin and took responsibility for his actions. Grace prevailed as God intervened and stopped the angel from striking the people further.

Jonah and the city of Nineveh –

God withheld His judgment and showed grace by changing His mind, as the people repented of their sins and sought the Lord.

Jonah (although an angel is not mentioned) was sent to preach to Nineveh, announcing that God would destroy the city in forty days.

But the people responded to Jonah when he preached and repented of their evil ways.

"So, the people of Nineveh believed God, proclaimed a fast, and put on sackcloth, from the greatest to the least of them."…. "Then God saw

their works, that they turned from their evil way, and God relented from the disaster that He had said He would bring upon them and He did not do it." Jonah 3:5 and 10.

The power of one angel

The prophet Isaiah delivers God's message to King Hezekiah of Judah, assuring him that the king of Assyria, Sennacherib, would not enter Jerusalem, shoot an arrow there, or besiege it.

"Therefore, thus says the Lord concerning the king of Assyria: "He shall not come into this city, nor shoot an arrow there, nor come before it with shield, nor build a siege mound against it." 2 Kings 19:32.

The prophecy was fulfilled by God sending an angel (only one is mentioned) who struck down and killed 185,000 Assyrian soldiers.

"And it came to pass on a certain night that the angel of the Lord went out, and killed in the camp of the Assyrians one hundred and eighty-five thousand; and when people arose early in the morning, there were the corpses – all dead." 2 Kings 19:35.

We are not told how the angel managed to kill so many. However, the king of Assyria fled to Nineveh. While he was worshipping in the temple of his god Nisroch, in Nineveh, his sons assassinated him with the sword.

King Herod and an angel of judgment

An angel struck down King Herod. (Which one?)

"So, on a set day, King Herod (Agrippa), arrayed in royal apparel, sat

on his throne and gave an oration to them. And the people kept shouting, "The voice of a god and not of a man." Then, immediately, an angel of the Lord struck him, because he did not give glory to God. And he was eaten by worms and died. But the word of God grew and multiplied." Matthew 12:21-23.

Someone is bound to ask, as I did, which King Herod this refers to. There are four that form a dynasty in the New Testament, and it can be confusing to work out which one it is. I will outline each of them.

1. Herod the Great (ruled 37-4 BC)

He was king when Jesus was born. He ordered the massacre of infants in Bethlehem. He died shortly after Jesus' birth (Matthew 2:1-20).

2. Herod Antipas (ruled 4 BC-AD 39)

Son of Herod the Great. Ruled as tetrarch of Galilee and Perea. He ordered the execution of John the Baptist (Mark 6:17-28). Pilate sent Jesus to him during the trial (Luke 23:6-12).

3. Herod Agrippa 1 (ruled AD 37-44)

Grandson of Herod the Great. Persecuted the early church and executed James. He arrested Peter. He was struck dead by an angel. (the one in our reference above) (Acts 12:1-23).

4. Herod Agrippa 2 (ruled AD 50s-93)

Son of Herod Agrippa 1. He heard Paul's defence before Festus. He said to Paul, "You almost persuaded me to become a Christian" (Acts 25:13, 26:32).

King Nebuchadnezzar and an angel

The King had a dream in which a "watcher" (an angelic being) judges him in a vision.

"I saw in the visions in my head while on my bed, and there was a watcher, a holy one, coming down from heaven." Daniel 4:13.

Without going into detail, the angel reveals an interesting vision, which Daniel interprets as a warning to Nebuchadnezzar that he would lose his mind, be driven from his throne, and live like an animal grazing on grass until he acknowledged God's sovereignty. It happened just as Daniel had interpreted the dream. After some time, he came to his senses.

"And at the end of the time I, Nebuchadnezzar, lifted my eyes to heaven, and my understanding returned to me, and I blessed the Most-High and praised and honoured Him who lives forever: for His dominion is an everlasting dominion, and His kingdom is from generation to generation." Daniel 4:34.

In conclusion, angels often act in judgment to uphold God's holiness and purity, ensuring that sin does not go unpunished. In this way, they maintain order and justice in God's kingdom and help administer the universe so that God's will is carried out.

Chapter 11

How do we compare with angels?

"What is man that You are mindful of him, and the son of man that You visit him? For You have made him a little lower than the angels, and You have crowned him with glory and honour."

Psalm 8:4-5.

David asks, *"What is man that You are mindful of him?"* The above scripture is not only prophetic of Christ but also of redeemed humanity. What is man in the context of the entire creation?

God knows we are but a speck of dust. "For He knows our frame; He remembers that we are dust." Psalm 103:14. God formed us from the dust of the earth, so we were made a little lower than the angels.

In our human weakness, why is God even mindful of us?

Although God formed us from the dust, He created us in His own image.

"So, God created man in His own image; in the image of God, He created him; male and female, He created them. Then God blessed them, and God said to them, "Be fruitful and multiply; fill the earth and subdue it; have dominion over the fish of the sea, over the birds of the air, and over every living thing that moves on the earth." Genesis 2:27-28.

We may begin a little lower than the angels, but we are uniquely created in the image of God, whereas angels are not. However, despite our physical limitations and mortality, we have been given dominion over the earth. Angels are not given that privilege, even though they are eternal, powerful, and spiritual beings.

Yet, God chose to crown Jesus and redeem man with glory and honour far above the angels. No, it is not a contradiction. It allows for our redemption and transformation through salvation in Christ.

We were created as mortals in weakness and confined to frail human bodies of flesh and blood that will experience pain and suffering and finally death before entering into eternal life in heaven.

So, David asks why God is mindful of man and willing to redeem him and adopt him into His own family.

Derek Kidner quotes in Tyndale Old Testament Commentaries, "The psalmist stands amazed that the God who set the stars in place would take notice of frail humanity.

Yet, astonishingly, mankind is given a status only slightly below that of the heavenly beings and crowned with divine honour.

When Jesus took on human form, He, too, was made a little lower than the angels. He became a man, not an angel.

"But we see Jesus, who was made a little lower than the angels, for the suffering of death crowned with glory and honour, that He, by the grace of God, might taste death for everyone." Hebrews 2:9.

Jesus had to become flesh and blood to die on the cross for the redemption of mankind. To do this, He became a little lower than angels until His resurrection and ascension.

Man has a higher status in eternity

It is thought that redeemed mankind will have a higher status than angels in eternity and will have a far more meaningful relationship with God as sons and daughters belonging to the family of God throughout eternity. Redeemed, man, is eventually crowned with glory and honour. Some claim that Satan's hatred for humans is borne out of his jealousy of our elevated status. Wendy Alec, who wrote The Fall of Lucifer, emphasises this concept.

1. *Angels do not call God their Father –*

"For to which of the angels did He ever say: You are My Son, Today I have begotten you?" I will be to him, a Father, and he shall be to me a Son." Hebrews 1:5.

Jesus said to His disciples My Father and Your Father. Christians have the right to refer to God as their Father.

"I am ascending to My Father and to your Father, and to My God and to your God." John 20:17.

2. We become Joint heirs with Jesus –

Christians are adopted into the family of God to become joint heirs with Jesus.

"For you did not receive the spirit of bondage again to fear, but you received the Spirit of adoption by whom we cry out, "Abba, Father" "The Spirit itself bears witness with our Spirit that we are children of God, and if children, then heirs – heirs of God and joint heirs with Christ. Romans 8:14-17.

3. We will reign with Christ –

The Bible indicates that we will reign with Christ. Determining what that will look like is difficult, as we do not receive a detailed picture. *"If we endure, we shall also reign with Him."* 2 Timothy 2:12.

We also read in Revelation 22:5, speaking of the redeemed in heaven, *"There shall be no night there; they need no lamp nor light of the sun, for the Lord God gives them light. And they shall reign forever and ever."* Revelation 22:5

4. Christians will judge Angels –

We are not sure how this will happen, but it validates the status of humans over angels in eternity. *"Do you not know that the saints will judge the world? And if you will judge the world, are you unworthy to judge the most minor matters? Do you not know that we shall judge angels?"* 1 Corinthians 6:2-3.

For your interest, we often discuss meeting up with friends, relatives, and fellow Christians in heaven and sharing fellowship with them.

I wonder if we will develop relationships with angels that perhaps observed our Christian journey on earth. Maybe they will tell us how we kept them busy and what they did for us. Perhaps they will recount historical events that have occurred.

"Are they not all ministering spirits sent forth to minister for those who will inherit salvation?" (Hebrews 1:14).

This may indicate an ongoing relationship in eternity. There is no indication of the depth that it may take, but it is food for thought.

We will worship God together with the angels

Angels are not omnipresent, meaning they are not everywhere present at the same time. They serve God as messengers and are busy worldwide as God orders them.

But they also spend a lot of time worshipping God before the throne of God, adoring their creator. Although we may differ from angels in many ways, there is one thing we will all do together with angels throughout eternity: Worship God.

Thomas Aquinas said, "The whole life of the Church is a preparation for the eternal worship of God, in which men and angels shall glorify Him without end" (Summa Theologica, Part 1, Q. 106).

We were in a new church auditorium set in five acres of

bushland on the outskirts of Melbourne. I was an assistant pastor at the time. It was a lovely sunny Sunday morning; the place was packed with people, and we were in a time of praise and worship.

I slipped outside to see if the car park was full. It was like I had stepped into heaven. It was the most beautiful sound I had ever heard. You could listen to the worship, and all the birds in the trees had joined in, and I am sure some of the angels had joined in as well. It was so glorious that I was reluctant to go back inside.

It would be awesome if that were a foretaste of what to expect in heaven. I could not help but think of the last verse of Psalm 150. "Let everything that has breath praise the Lord."

John Wesley says, "Our worship on earth is but a rehearsal for the grand chorus of praise where angels and redeemed men shall magnify the Lamb together."

"After these things, I looked, and behold, a great multitude which no one could number, of all nations, tribes, peoples, tongues, standing before the throne and before the Lamb, clothed with white robes, with palm branches in their hands, and crying out with a loud voice, saying, "Salvation belongs to our God who sits on the throne and to the Lamb!" All the angels stood around the throne and the elders and the four living creatures, and fell on their faces before the throne and worshipped God, saying, "Amen! Blessing and glory and wisdom, thanksgiving and honour and power and might be to our God forever and ever, Amen." Revelation 7:9-12.

The above passage explicitly shows the redeemed believers

and angels worshipping God together in heaven. Worship will not be a competition between men and angels in heaven; it will be a glorious harmony that magnifies the Lord.

In a paraphrase from his sermon *The Weight of Glory*, C.S. Lewis states, "Heaven is not a place where we are separate from angels, but where we shall join them in the great dance of worship before the throne of God."

DO ANGELS WALK AMONG US TODAY?

Chapter 12

Angels as providers and protectors

"Then, as he lay and slept under a broom tree, suddenly an angel touched him; and said to him, "Arise and eat." Then he looked, and there by his head was a cake baked on coals, and a jar of water. So, he ate and drank and lay down again."

1 Kings 19:5-6

The angel provided Elijah with a cake baked on coals and a jar of water. He was fleeing for his life after killing the prophets of Baal. King Ahab and his wife, Jezebel, had worshipped Baal, not the Lord.

Elijah had built an altar and challenged the prophets of Baal to call down fire from heaven. Whoever answers by fire and lights the altar is the true God. The prophets of Baal failed, but Elijah called on the Lord. And He answered by fire, consuming the altar.

Then Elijah killed all the prophets of Baal.

Instead of Ahab and Jezebel turning to the Lord, they were furious and sought to kill Elijah. Jezebel sent a message to Elijah, telling him he would be dead like one of the prophets of Baal by this time tomorrow. So, Elijah fled into the wilderness and was afraid, distressed and depressed, so he prayed that he might die and said,

"It is enough! Now, Lord, take my life, for I am no better than my fathers." 1 Kings 19:4.

However, the Lord sent an angel who provided them with food and drink. But after Elijah ate and drank, he lay down again. So, the angel returned the second time, touched him and said,

"Arise and eat because the journey is too great for you." So, he arose and ate and drank and he went in the strength of that food forty days and forty nights as far as Horeb, the mountain of God." (V 7-8).

The point is that angels provided for and protected Elijah on this occasion. After God had dealt with Elijah, who was sheltering in a cave at Horeb, He sent him on a mission and directed him to resume his prophetic role, to go and anoint Hazael as king over Syria, anoint Jehu as king over Israel, and anoint Elisha as prophet in his place.

During World War 2

American soldiers sought shelter in an abandoned monastery near Monte Cassino, Italy.

As they huddled together, fearing an attack, they heard the sound of monks chanting. A group of robed men entered the room, offering them bread and water. They quickly fell asleep.

The monks were gone when they awoke, and the monastery once again appeared empty. Locals later told them that the monastery had been deserted for years. They believe angels visited them.

The late Billy Graham

Billy was a renowned evangelist who impacted nations for decades, leading countless people to follow Christ.

In his book *Angels: God's Secret Agents,* he recounts, "I have often felt too spent to minister from the pulpit to the men and women who have filled stadiums to hear a message from the Lord."

"Yet, again and again, my weariness has vanished, and my strength has been renewed. God has sent His unseen angelic visitors to touch my body to let me be his messenger for heaven, speaking as a dying man to dying men."

Some possible personal encounters

I cannot prove that some encounters were angels, so I use the word "possible." Besides, Jesus said, "All things are possible with God."

The provision of fish bait -

As a family, we were holidaying in the beautiful Whitsunday

Islands. We had hired a thirty-five-foot Cruiser. My son Andrew was a teenager (now a Baptist minister who has helped me with all my books) and, like me, a keen fisherman. We always seem to be running out of bait. We casually prayed about it. On one occasion, we were anchored in a lovely inlet with no bait, and when we came up on deck in the morning, several squid were on it. With God's help, something must have caused them to jump on board

On another occasion, we were anchored in a lovely, quiet cove. That night, we heard a lot of splashing around the boat, thinking that the fish were being chased by something. To our surprise, the next morning, when we went to get in our dinghy to go ashore, there were baitfish all over it. Was it the work of Angels, or did God order some dolphins to flick up bait fish into the dinghy?

I thought of the scripture where an Angel would sometimes stir up the water at the pool of Bethesda, and the first one to get into the pool after the angel had stirred the waters would be healed. (John 5:4).

Somehow, the Lord had stirred up the waters, causing the fish to leap onto the boat. Thank you, Lord!

Financial provision on the mission field –

We were acutely aware of God's miraculous provision and protection while serving on the mission field in Papua New Guinea (PNG). We spent six years in PNG, but after the first year, our home church in Melbourne withdrew its financial support because I had initially stated that I would return after one year. However, I needed to stay longer to establish the Bible College we had started. As soon as the support was withdrawn, we suddenly began to receive sufficient support through the mail from two widows in the church to get us by until a church in Brisbane, led by the late Trevor Chandler, supported us for another five years while we were in PNG. The mail system was corrupt and unreliable, so we wonder if angels helped with the delivery.

Protection on the mission field -

In the city of Port Moresby, the crime rate was horrendous. There were lots of rascal gangs (a rascal in English is thought to be someone naughty), but these gangs were often led by hardened criminals responsible for stealing, break-ins, rape, and murder.

We had a high fence around our home covered in Bougainvillea (flowers with spikes) and security lights at night. My wife had gone to Australia with our baby daughter and son to visit her dying mother. One night, I had to go and lecture in our night Bible school, which was about seventy meters away on the same property, and leave the two school-age girls on their own. They had an old bell from a ship we had set up in the lounge room. I told them to ring it if there was a problem. I was about half an hour into my lecture when the bell rang. I immediately dropped everything and ran, with several Bible school students following behind me. When we got inside, the girls were terrified because a small gang of rascals had surrounded the house and started dismantling our louvres to break in just as the girls rang the bell. The girls said the gang members tried to step inside but could not enter the house. We believe angels had protected them.

Protection from Malaria on the mission field -

We were very thankful as a family during our six years in PNG that none of us contracted Malaria. We took tablets and avoided mosquito bites, a common occurrence in Papua New Guinea (PNG).

I was exposed to Mosquitoes trudging through mud in jungles, crossing rivers, and living in villages. I was careful, but was bitten many times. Whenever I saw or felt a mosquito, I would try to swat it. Maybe some unseen angels were also swatting them on my behalf. I would not have been surprised if I had succumbed to Malaria or one of our family, but thank God we were all protected.

Not to mention the stories of God's protection from hostile tribes, deadly snakes, sharks, and crocodiles while ministering in various areas of PNG.

God uses an angel to protect Israel

Israel was escaping from Egypt, being pursued by the Egyptians, and was ultimately led by Moses to the shores of the Red Sea.

"And the angel of God, who went before the camp of Israel, moved and went behind them; and the pillar of cloud went from before them and

stood behind them. So, it came before the camp of the Egyptians and the camp of Israel. Thus, it was a cloud and darkness to one, and it gave light by night to the other, so that the one did not come near the other all night." Exodus 14:19-20.

The next day, God opened the Red Sea, and Moses led the Israelites to the other side. When the Egyptians pursued them in chariots, God closed the waters of the Red Sea, and the Egyptians drowned.

God sustains Israel with angels' food

God sustained the entire nation of Israel, providing them with supernatural food in the wilderness.

"God rained down manna on them to eat, and gave them the bread of heaven. Men ate angels' food; He sent them food to the full." Psalm 78:24-25.

In Exodus, we have more information about this food that sustained a nation in the wilderness.

"Then the Lord said to Moses, "Behold, I will rain bread from heaven for you, and the people shall go out and gather a certain quota every day, that I may test them, whether they will walk in My law or not."…. "And the house of Israel called its name; Manna. And it was like white coriander seed, and the taste of it was like wafers made with honey." Exodus 16:4,31.

Although God provided the manna, the Israelites were still responsible for gathering it daily. They were to gather enough for each household and were not allowed to hoard it; it had to be fresh. Additionally, they were required to collect a double portion on the sixth day, allowing them to rest and worship God on the seventh day. It reminds me of what Jesus asks Christians to pray as part of the Lord's prayer: *"Give us this day our daily bread"* (Matthew 6:11).

From a spiritual perspective, we cannot expect God or angels to spoon-feed us. Christians are responsible for sustaining themselves through the Word of God, the Holy Spirit, and fellowship. But God can still intervene if He so desires.

Saint Francis of Assisi was renowned for his profound spirituality and deep affection for the poor; he reportedly encountered an angel who provided comfort and guidance. There are also accounts of times when he fasted and prayed and was miraculously sustained by divine means.

Chapter 13

Are angels church spectators?

> *"For it seems to me that God has made an exhibit of us apostles, exposing us to view last (of all like men in a triumphal procession who are) sentenced to death (and displayed at the end of the line). For we have become a spectacle to the world – a show in the world's amphitheatre – with both men and angels (as spectators)."*

1 Corinthians 4:9 (AMP).

In the above verse (9), Paul wears his heart on his sleeve and describes how the apostles, including himself, are treated with dishonour and suffer for the sake of the gospel before men and angels.

He compares their position to that of prisoners condemned to death, much like gladiators or criminals displayed in Roman arenas for a public spectacle.

The Greek word for "spectacle" is theatron, which suggests a theatrical display; in this context, it refers to observing earthly humans and spiritual beings as they suffer. Both men and angels are witnesses to the endurance of their faith. However, it also implies that God restrains both from intervening or acting to deliver them.

Why does God sometimes restrain angels?

Sometimes, we must understand that God tests our faith and endurance, allowing us to suffer conflict without intervening. Therefore, it would seem that God sometimes restrains angels from rushing in to rescue us.

I have been asked many times about why God allows suffering. This isn't easy to answer. I see from a theological point of view that suffering relates to adverse circumstances and persecution, but I am reluctant to say, as many Christians do, that God uses sickness to test our faith. This would seem to contradict the nature of Jesus, his compassion for healing people, and the tone of scripture.

However, it seems the Lord turned a blind eye to Paul while battling his thorn in the flesh and prayed for it to be removed. Worse still, it was described as a messenger from Satan to keep him somehow humble.

The only answer Paul received from God was, *"My grace is sufficient for you, for My strength is made perfect in weakness."* 2 Corinthians 11:2-9.

Perhaps this is the only answer we need regarding suffering and the complex theological issues it raises.

When Jesus was on the cross, the angels would have been spectators waiting for a signal from Jesus or a command from the Father to rescue Him. But none came; it was not God's will. Jesus had to taste death for every man and shed His blood for the redemption of our sins.

"Do you think that I cannot now pray to My Father, and He will provide Me with more than twelve legions of angels?" Matthew 26:53.

In the Book of Hebrews, we read of a great crowd of witnesses surrounding us, much like the crowds at an arena. Mainly comprised of saints and, no doubt, angels watching, ready to help but restrained, because they need to see how, by faith, we endure trials and hostility from sinners. We are encouraged to focus on Jesus, our example.

"Looking unto Jesus, the author and finisher of our faith, who for the joy that was set before Him endured the cross, despising the shame, and has sat down at the right hand of the throne of God. For consider Him who endured such hostility from sinners against Himself, lest you become weary and discouraged in your souls." Hebrews 12:2-3.

The implication is that if Jesus endured the cross, despising its shame and humiliation, we can surely endure whatever we might be going through in life for the sake of the gospel. The incentive for us is that just as Jesus knew the joy before Him (to return to His throne in heaven). Then we, too, can look forward to the joy of our reward in heaven. So, let's give the spectators, both human and angelic in the stands of heaven, something to cheer about.

Angels observing the church

In his book, *Though I Walk Through the Valley,* Dr. Vance Havner tells the story of an old preacher who worked well into the night preparing his sermon for his small congregation.

His wife wondered why he spent so much time crafting a message that would be given to so few people. He replied, "You forget, my dear, how large my audience will be!" "Nothing is trivial here on earth if heaven is looking on. You never know who will be in the grandstand."

Over the centuries, angels have been said to watch over the Christian Church, observing its establishment and expansion worldwide despite opposition and persecution.

C. S. Lewis, in his *Screwtape Letters,* writes from a demon's perspective. "I see the enemy's angels standing guard about the wretched little church, their presence an unbearable light to us, their swords drawn lest we draw too close"

As spectators, angels are amazed at the unfolding wisdom of God that is now being revealed through the church as the gospel of Christ is preached. Angels are watching; they miss nothing but only act when God gives the order.

"To the intent that the manifold wisdom of God might be made known by the church to the principalities and powers in heavenly places." Ephesians 3:10.

The *"angels"* of the seven churches in Revelation chapters 2-3. As mentioned earlier in this book, the Greek word for *"angel,"* Angelos, means *"messenger,"* which in this case can refer to either a heavenly angel or a human messenger.

Some believe these angels are literal angels assigned to watch over the churches, while others believe these angels are human messengers, such as church leaders, pastors or bishops. This view holds that Jesus has entrusted these ministers with the church's responsibility. It is the most widespread belief and fits in with leaders being accountable for their people. (Hebrews 13:17). Perhaps it is both!

Whatever the case may be, angels, as spectators, are undoubtedly interested in the development and progress of the church.

Frank Peretti writes in his fictional but influential book, *This Present Darkness*, "Above the town, unseen by human eyes, angelic warriors stood as sentinels, their eyes fixed upon the little church where prayers ascended like incense, summoning divine aid against the encroaching darkness."

"I Jesus have sent My angel to testify to you these things in the churches." Revelation 22:16.

This particular angel is not mentioned, but it is the same one throughout the book that helped John see and understand the visions written for the church's benefit. Interpreting these visions is a challenge.

Paul writes to Timothy, *"I charge you before God and the Lord Jesus Christ and the elect angels that you observe these things without prejudice, doing nothing with partiality."* 1 Timothy 5: 21.

The implication is that God, Jesus and the angels are watching, and they are witnesses to this charge he gives Timothy.

Angels as spectators and participators

Watchman Nee, in his book, *The Spiritual Man*, says, "The church, being the body of Christ, is surrounded by spiritual forces – both angels and demons – who war over its purity and purpose. Yet the angels stand ever ready to defend His people."

Drawing on his experience and challenges, Paul knew that angels were both spectators and participants in helping believers and those like himself in ministry. As an apostle, he had every right to feel like a spectacle in an arena.

"In labours more abundant, in stripes above measure, in prisons more frequently, in deaths often. From the Jews, five times, I received forty stripes minus one. Three times I was beaten with rods; once I was stoned; three times I was shipwrecked; a night and a day I have been in the deep; in journeys often, in perils of water, in perils of robbers, in perils of my own countrymen, in perils of the Gentiles, in perils in the city, in perils in the wilderness, in perils in the sea, in perils among false brethren; in weariness and toil, in sleeplessness often, in hunger and thirst, in fasting's often, in cold and nakedness – besides the other things, what comes upon me daily; my deep concern for the churches." 2 Corinthians 11:23-28.

Seriously, who wants to be an apostle after reading through that list? The angels were spectators most of the time. I'm sure we feel the same way when we go through times when our faith is being tested. However, Paul occasionally encountered angels who came to his rescue.

The most notable appearance of an angel to Paul occurred when he was on a ship caught in a storm. He encouraged everyone by saying,

"And now I urge you to take heart, for there will be no loss of life among you, but only of the ship." For there stood by me this night an angel of God to whom I belong and to whom I serve, saying, "Do not be afraid, Paul; you must be brought before Caesar; and indeed, God has granted you all those who sail with you. Therefore, take heart men, for I believe God that it will be just as it was told me." Acts 27:22-25.

The ship was wrecked, but Paul and all those on board were saved just as the angel had told him.

There are other possible instances. Paul and Silas were supernaturally released from prison due to a great earthquake.

"Suddenly there was a great earthquake, so that the foundations of the prison were shaken; and immediately all the doors were opened and everyone's chains were loosed." Acts 16:26.

Although an angel is not mentioned, they may have been involved. Paul led the jailer to the Lord, then preached the gospel to his family, and all who heard him were baptised. The next day, the magistrates decided to release Paul. Additionally, when Paul was supernaturally caught up to the third heaven and in Paradise, he heard inexpressible words, which were not lawful for a man to utter; he probably would have encountered angels or possibly overheard them discussing sacred matters (2 Corinthians 12:2-4). In the life of Paul and the early church, it is clear that angels were both spectators and participants, as God commanded them to be.

Angels are sent to minister to believers by watching over them, protecting them, delivering them, and guiding them. (Psalm 91:11, Hebrews 1:14).

This raises the question. Do we have personal guardian angels who are assigned to us?

There is a possibility that Acts 12:15 and Matthew 18:10 may support this interpretation. Whatever the case may be, we are very thankful for their ministry.

Chapter 14

The Holy Spirit reigns over all angels

"Therefore, I say to you, every sin and blasphemy will be forgiven men, but the blasphemy against the Spirit will not be forgiven men." ....
"Whoever speaks against the Holy Spirit, it will not be forgiven him, either in this age or the age to come."

Matthew 12: 31-32

The above scripture says, "Blasphemy against the Holy Spirit will not be forgiven." But there is no such statement in the Bible about blaspheming angels, which highlights the Holy Spirit's superior status. The Holy Spirit, as God, rules over all the angels.

R. C. Sproul, an American theologian, pastor, and founder of *Ligonier Ministries*, says, "The Holy Spirit does not draw attention to Himself. He always points to the Son. He is more significant than angels, for He is God, the third person of the Trinity.

Someone once said, "How can you believe in the Trinity, because the word Trinity is not in the Bible?" That may be true, but the Bible opens with the Triune Godhead, as referred to in Genesis 1:1-3, comprising God the Father, the Holy Spirit, and the Word (Jesus the Son), as confirmed in John 1:1-3.

Blaspheming the Holy Spirit deliberately and wilfully rejects the Spirit's work that glorifies Jesus as Lord. Jesus performed miracles by the power of the Holy Spirit, whereas the Pharisees said it was by the power of Satan.

Why is this unforgivable? The Holy Spirit is to convict people of sin and reveal the forgiveness of Christ so they can repent and turn to Christ as their Saviour and Lord. (John 16:8-11). To blaspheme Christ is like a hardening of the arteries; it is a permanent rejection of God's grace and mercy that leads to spiritual and eternal rejection.

This blasphemy is not a one-time mistake but a continual, hardened, and unrepentant resistance to the Holy Spirit throughout one's lifetime.

Billy Graham, in his book, *The Holy Spirit: Activating God's Power in Your Life*, states, "The Holy Spirit does what no angel can – He convicts, regenerates, and sanctifies. He is not a mere servant of God; He is God Himself at work."

We should be cautious of preachers and ministries who claim to be acting on instructions from angels rather than the Holy Spirit.

The Holy Spirit and the working of miracles

In the Gospels, the Book of Acts, and the epistles, the Holy Spirit imparts life and is responsible for all kinds of creative miracles that overshadow the work of angels.

In his book *The Counsellor*, A.A. Tozer says, "The Holy Spirit, being God, is infinitely superior to angels. While they serve, He commands; while they minister, He empowers."

"Jesus said, The Spirit of the Lord is upon Me to preach the gospel to the poor; He has sent Me to heal the broken hearted, to proclaim liberty to the captives and recovery of sight to the blind, to set at liberty those that are oppressed; to proclaim the acceptable year of the Lord." Luke 4:18.

As confirmation of the above scripture, we read in Acts 10:38, *"How God anointed Jesus of Nazareth with the Holy Spirit and with power who went about doing good and healing all those who were oppressed by the devil, for God was with Him."*

The apostles attributed the working of miracles, signs and wonders to the power of the Holy Spirit.

"And through the hands of the apostles, many signs and wonders were done among the people."…. *"So, they brought the sick out into the streets and laid them on beds and couches so that at least the shadow of Peter passing by might fall on some of them. Also, a multitude gathered from the surrounding cities to Jerusalem, bringing sick people and those who were tormented by unclean spirits, and they were all healed."* Acts 5: 13-16.

Kathryn Kulman and the Holy Spirit

Kathryn was a famous evangelist with a powerful healing ministry; she did not focus on angels. However, she was aware of their presence; she focused on the miracle-working power of the Holy Spirit throughout her ministry.

She says, "I believe in miracles because I believe in God." "The Holy Spirit is more real to me than you are." "The Holy Spirit is my best friend."

There is minimal teaching, if any, by Kathryn Kuhlman on angels. Unlike some ministries that emphasise personal encounters with angels, Kuhlman warned against making angels the centre of attention. She focused on the Holy Spirit and giving all the glory to God.

Kathryn once said, "I understand what David meant when He cried out to God, "Do not cast me away from your presence, and do not take your Holy Spirit from me." (Palm 51:11)

Kathryn said, "I fear no man, demon or the devil. The only thing I fear is losing the anointing of the Holy Spirit."

Jesus said the Holy Spirit would replace Him

In his book *The Pursuit of God*, American pastor and author A.W. Tozer states, "The idea that the Holy Spirit is an impersonal influence or power that we are somehow to grasp and utilise is a completely false and pagan notion." The Holy Spirit is a person who takes hold of us and uses us.

On several occasions, Jesus told His disciples that He would return to His Father, but promised to send another Helper, the Holy Spirit, to comfort and guide them into all truth.

"And I will pray to the Father, and He will give you another Helper, that He may abide with you forever – the Spirit of truth, whom the world cannot receive; because it neither sees Him nor knows Him; but you know Him, for He dwells with you and shall be in you. I will not leave you orphans; I will come to you." John 14:15-18.

We are not alone, wandering around like lost sheep without a purpose. We are now being led and guided by the Holy Spirit. Yes, the Holy Spirit is our helper throughout this church age, and we need to depend on Him to lead and guide us.

"But the Helper, the Holy Spirit, whom the Father will send in My name. He will teach you all things and bring to your remembrance all things that I have said to you." John 14:25.

Jesus told his disciples that He would guide them into all truth and glorify Christ when the Holy Spirit came. This applies to all believers throughout the church age.

He (the Holy Spirit) will glorify Me, for He will take of what is Mine and declare it to you. All things that the Father has are Mine. Therefore, I said, *"That He will take of Mine and declare it to you."* John 16:14-15. By doing this, the Holy Spirit will reveal truth, and only glorify Jesus.

The Holy Spirit empowers believers

The Holy Spirit empowers believers, not angels.

An English theologian, *John Owen*, says, "The Holy Spirit is not given to us to do a work that angels could do. He is given to us for a work that neither men nor angels can do – He alone can create us anew in Christ. Jesus wanted his disciples to be empowered by the Holy Spirit. Before He ascended, He said to them.

"Behold, I send the promise of My Father upon you, but tarry in the city of Jerusalem until you are endued with power from on high." Luke 24:49.

Jesus was referring to the initial outpouring of the Holy Spirit on the Day of Pentecost. The phrase means to be clothed or equipped with divine power, enabling them to preach the gospel, perform miracles, and live victoriously.

In another reference, just before He ascended, Jesus said, *"You shall receive power when the Holy Spirit has come upon you, and you shall be witnesses to Me in Jerusalem, and in all Judea and Samaria, and to the end of the earth."* Acts 1:8.

Jesus is again speaking of the power of the Holy Spirit to be poured out in Jerusalem on the Day of Pentecost, enabling them to be witnesses, beginning in Jerusalem and then spreading the gospel to the ends of the earth.

Is this power still available today? It certainly is! When I was baptised in the Holy Spirit, like on the Day of Pentecost, with the evidence of speaking in tongues, it transformed my life. It empowered me to walk in the Spirit and believe in the supernatural power and gifts of the Holy Spirit. I felt more equipped as a Christian and had a greater desire to train for the ministry.

I shared my newfound understanding with the Presbyterian minister at the church where I attended Sunday school. He was not impressed and felt it no longer applies to us today.

The pastor of the Church of Christ, who married us, became very upset when we told him we had enrolled in a Charismatic Bible College to train for the ministry. He strongly advised us not to attend because Pentecost was no longer a valid experience for today.

Despite the negatives, we went ahead, and in retrospect, it was the best thing for us at the time.

How can you be endured with power today?

*Desire and seek the Holy Spirit – *"How much more will your Father give the Holy Spirit to those who ask him."* Luke 11:13.

The Holy Spirit at work in the church

Augustine of Hippo (Saint Augustine), a theologian and philosopher, said, "What the soul is to the human body, the Holy Spirit is the body of Christ, which is the church." The Holy Spirit should supernaturally empower the church.

How true that is! Without the Holy Spirit, the church lacks soul (life and power) and is no more than just another organisation doing good in the community. But has little impact on changing lives through the gospel's transforming power.

***Born again by the Spirit* –**

When Nicodemus, a ruler of the Jews, came to Jesus by night, declaring that Jesus was a teacher sent from God, Jesus said, "Unless one is born again, he cannot see the kingdom of God."

When Nicodemus protested that it was not possible to be born again when you are old, Jesus answered, "That which is born of the flesh is flesh, and that which is born of the Spirit is spirit. Do not marvel that I said to you, you must be born again." (John 3:1-7). This happens when we receive Christ as our Saviour and Lord.

***Gifts of the Holy Spirit* -**

God, not angels, has given the church spiritual gifts for the edification of the body of Christ, the church. Paul explains how these gifts work in the context of the church.

"Now, concerning spiritual gifts, brethren, I do not want you to be ignorant."…. "There are diversities of gifts, but the same Spirit. There are differences of ministries, but the same Lord. And there are diversities of activities, but it is the same God who works all in all." 1 Corinthians 12:1-6.

Paul expounds on the gifts of the Spirit and their purpose. He tells us that each person operating a gift does so to edify the church so that everyone benefits from it.

He lists nine spiritual gifts: a word of wisdom, a word of knowledge, faith, healings, the working of miracles, prophecy, the discerning of spirits, tongues, and the interpretation of tongues.

Different believers operate them, but they all come from the Holy Spirit.

Walking in the Spirit -

We are told that the Holy Spirit helps believers in the church to walk in the Spirit so that we do not fulfil the lusts of the flesh.

"Walk in the Spirit, and you shall not fulfil the lust of the flesh." Galatians 5:16.

This is written in the context where Paul lists the works of the flesh and the fruit of the Spirit. We are encouraged to walk in the Spirit, as evidenced by the fruit of the Spirit, which includes love, joy, peace, patience, kindness, goodness, faithfulness, gentleness, and self-control. (Galatians 5:22-23).

Divine revelation by the Spirit –

Angels carry messages, and the Spirit gives revelation concerning the deep things of God. He reveals the truth and helps us distinguish between deception and reality.

"However, when He, the Spirit of Truth, has come, He will guide you into all truth." John 16:13.

"These things God has revealed to us by the Holy Spirit." 1 Corinthians 2:10-11.

"For prophecy never came by the will of man, but holy men of God spoke as they were moved by the Holy Spirit." 1 Peter 1:21.

Praying in the Spirit –

The Holy Spirit helps us pray in accordance with God's will. Sometimes, we struggle with prayer and are unsure how to articulate our thoughts, what to ask for, or how to ask. We are told we can intercede with groanings that cannot be uttered.

"Likewise, the Spirit also helps in our weaknesses. For we do not know how to pray as we ought, but the Spirit Himself intercedes for us with groanings that cannot be expressed. Now, He, who searches the hearts, knows what the mind of the Spirit is; because He makes intercession for the saints according to the will of God." Romans 8:26-27.

The Holy Spirit seals our salvation –

The Holy Spirit guarantees our salvation. It signifies that we belong to God, and external forces cannot break the seal of the Holy Spirit until our redemption is complete.

"In Him you also trusted, after you heard the word of truth, the gospel of your salvation; in whom also having believed, you were sealed with the Holy Spirit of promise." Ephesians 1:13.

The angels of God are to be admired, not worshipped. However, we are in awe of the Holy Spirit, who is part of the Trinity and is equal to God. The Holy Spirit must be given pre-eminence throughout this church age.

Chapter 15

An angel rolled the stone away

"Mary Magdalene and the other Mary came to see the tomb. And behold, there was a great earthquake; for an angel of the Lord descended from heaven, and came and rolled back the stone from the door and sat on it."

Matthew 28:1-2.

The scripture above shows that an angel rolled the stone away when Jesus rose from the dead. This was not to let Jesus out, for He had already risen; it was to show the disciples, the Romans, and the world that the tomb was empty because Jesus had risen as He said he would.

A Canadian Christian musician, *Carolyn Arends*, said, "My pastor said something that stopped me in my mental tracks: 'The world offers promises full of emptiness - But Easter offers emptiness full of promises.'

How true that is, often leading up to elections, some politicians make promises that ultimately lead to disappointment. But the empty tomb gives promises that lead to salvation, eternal life, and heaven.

The women on their way to the tomb, where they had laid Jesus, were met by an angel who told them, "He is not here; he is risen."

"But the angel answered and said to the women,' Do not be afraid, for I know you are seeking Jesus, who was crucified." "He is not here, for He has risen as He said. Come see the place where the Lord lay." Matthew 28:5-6.

The women were invited to view the empty tomb for themselves. However, on the way to the tomb, the women had wondered who would move the stone away, as it was huge, heavy, and sealed.

"And they said among themselves, "Who will roll away the stone from the door of the tomb for us?" But when they looked up, they saw the stone had been rolled away – for it was very large." Mark 16:3-4. (An angel had rolled away the stone.)

These stones, possibly in the shape of a large millstone, can weigh anywhere from one to two tons (2,000 to 4,000 pounds) — no problem for the supernatural strength of an angel.

Who put the stone there in the first place?

This raises the question of who rolled the stone there in the first place? We are told that Joseph of Arimathea came and sought permission to take the body of Jesus and lay it in his newly hewn tomb.

"Being a disciple of Jesus, but secretly for fear of the Jews, he asked Pilate that he might take away the body of Jesus; and Pilate gave him permission. So, he came and took the body of Jesus. And Nicodemus, who at first came to Jesus by night, also came, bringing a mixture of myrrh and aloes, about a hundred pounds. Then they took the body of Jesus, and bound it in strips of linen with the spices, as the custom of the Jews is to bury." John 19:38-40.

Joseph could not manage the body of Jesus on his own, so we know (from the above scripture) that he had Nicodemus. There may have been other disciples or even Roman soldiers who assisted in rolling the stone into place.

The stone was sealed and guarded

After the stone was set in place, the chief priests and Pharisees approached Pilate to persuade him to secure it so that no one could break in and steal the body and then claim that He had risen.

"The chief priests and Pharisees gathered together to Pilate, saying, "Sir, we remember, while He was still alive, how that deceiver said, "After three days I will rise." "Therefore, command that the tomb be made secure until the third day, lest His disciples come by night and steal Him away, and say to the people, "He has risen from the dead." "So, the last deception is worse than the first." Pilate said to them, "You have a guard; go your way, make it as secure as you know how." So, they went and made the tomb secure, sealing the stone and setting the guard".

Matthew 27:62-66. (The stone was possibly sealed with rope and wax, ensuring no one could break the seal and enter the tomb.)

When the angel came to roll the stone away, the subsequent earthquake likely broke the seal that secured the stone. When the soldiers guarding the tomb saw the angel, they were terrified. "His countenance was like lightning, and his clothing as white as snow. And the guards shook for fear of him and became like dead men." (Matthew 28:3-4).

Why is all this so important?

The empty tomb and the resurrection of Jesus are at the centre of our Christian faith. It is so crucial to Christianity, the apostle Paul said,

"If the dead do not rise, then Christ is not risen. And if Christ is not risen, your faith is futile; you are still in your sins!" 1 Corinthians 15:17.

Charles Spurgeon, often called the Prince of Preachers, frequently preached about how the resurrection is the foundation of the Christian faith. He saw the rolled-away stone as both a historical reality and a metaphor for removing sin and doubt, allowing believers to witness the power of God.

In his book Who Moved the Stone, Frank Morrison, a British journalist sceptical of the Christian faith, set out to prove that the resurrection was a myth.

Instead of disproving the resurrection, his research revealed compelling evidence that caused him to change his views. He became convinced of the authenticity of the resurrection and wrote his book, which has become a classic in Christian apologetics.

The main issue of his book revolves around the empty tomb and the mystery of what happened to Jesus's body. When Mary Magdalene looked into the tomb, she saw two angels, yet it is implied in Matthew that only one rolled the stone away.

"She saw two angels in white sitting, one at the head and the other at the feet, where the body of Jesus had lain. Then they said to her, "Woman, why are you weeping?" She said to them, "Because they have taken away my Lord, and I do not know where they have laid him." John 20:12-13.

She said, *"I do not know where they have laid Him."* This poses the question of where the body was and how it disappeared. Morrison was satisfied that the evidence for the resurrection was conclusive and was convinced that the stone, sealed and guarded by soldiers, could not have been moved without divine intervention. If the authorities of the day did not believe that Jesus had been raised from the dead, how would they explain the missing body? If He were dead, His body would have remained in the tomb.

The empty tomb and the resurrection of Jesus are the final proof for us as Christians that Jesus was who He claimed to be, the Son of God.

"They all asked, "Are you then the Son of God?" He replied, "You

are right in saying I am." Luke 22:70 (NIV).

As a result of the resurrection, let me outline several key facts that follow

Proof of Jesus' Divinity –

His resurrection validates His claim to be the Son of God, revealing His power over life and death.

Victory over sin and death –

By rising from the dead, Jesus conquered sin and death for all of humanity.

Assurance for all believers –

Jesus' resurrection is described as the first fruits, meaning those who believe in Him will also be raised from the dead.

The power of the Holy Spirit –

The same Spirit that raised Christ from the dead now dwells in believers, empowering them to serve Christ.

The establishment of the church –

After His resurrection, Jesus gave the Great Commission to His disciples, instructing them to go into all the world and preach the gospel to all nations.

The fulfilment of scripture –

After His resurrection, Jesus declared to His disciples.

"These are the words which I spoke to you while I was still with you, that all things must be fulfilled which were written in the law of Moses and the Prophets and the Psalms concerning me." And He opened their understanding that they might comprehend the scriptures. Then He said to them, "Thus it is written, and thus it was necessary for the Christ to suffer and to rise from the dead on the third day, and that repentance and remission of sins should be preached in His name to all nations, beginning at Jerusalem. And you are witnesses of these things." Luke 24:44-48.

The death, burial, and resurrection of Jesus were all prophesied in the scriptures beforehand and needed to be fulfilled for our redemption.

So, we see that God sent angels for the divine intervention necessary to roll away the stone and reveal an empty tomb, proving that Jesus had risen. Jesus appeared to many after His resurrection before He ascended to heaven.

DO ANGELS WALK AMONG US TODAY?

Chapter 16

The role of angels at Christ's return

"When the Son of Man comes in His glory, and all the holy angels with Him, then He will sit on the throne of His glory."

Matthew 25:31.

The above verse refers to the final judgment: Jesus, the Son of Man, returns in glory with His holy angels to claim His rightful place as King and Judge over all the nations on earth.

Despite some who mockingly say, "Where is His coming? It will happen; we do not get to vote, and it is not a debatable subject. Sometimes, God longs for something to happen, but He needs human cooperation to make it a reality. He gives us an option, so it may or may not occur. Regarding His return, your opinion does not matter; it is neither an option nor negotiable. It is an immutable promise, as stated in His word.

In his book, *The Second Coming*, John MacArthur says, "The

Lord's return will be marked by the presence of His mighty angels, executing divine justice and heralding the triumphant arrival of the King of Kings. Their role is not merely that of spectators but as active participants in the most significant event in human history, gathering the saints and pouring out judgment on the ungodly.

Watch and be ready

Are we ready for such a climactic finale? Nobody knows when this will happen, not even the angels; however, we are told to be watchful and prepared.

"But that day and hour, no one knows, not even the angels of heaven, but My Father only.".... "Watch, therefore, for you do not know what hour your Lord is coming."…. "Therefore, you also be ready for the Son of Man is coming at an hour you do not expect." Matthew 24:36, 42, 44.

The implication is that some will be caught off guard and unprepared because we do not know when this will happen. The Bible indicates it will be business as usual, just like in the days of Noah before the flood.

"For as in the days before the flood, they were eating and drinking, marrying and giving in marriage, until the day that Noah entered the ark, and did not know until the flood came and took them all away, so also will the coming of the Son of Man be." Matthew 24:38-39.

So, we are responsible for watching how we live in this world. The word watch means to be alert. Are we alert and living the way followers of Christ should be living? Are you ready for His return today?

Unfortunately, some will become impatient, cast off restraint, stop living like Christians, and align themselves with the ways of the world.

"But if the evil servant says in his heart, "My master is delaying His coming, and begins to beat his fellow servants, and to eat and drink with the drunkards, the master of that servant will come in a day when he is not looking for him, and at an hour he is not aware of." Matthew 24:49-50.

Angels promised He would return

The return of Christ to this earth is the fulfilment of a promise made by the angels to His disciples when Jesus ascended back to heaven.

"Now when He had spoken these things, while they watched, He was taken up, and a cloud received Him out of their sight. And while they looked steadfastly toward heaven as He went up, behold, two men stood by them in white apparel, who also said, "Men of Galilee, why do you stand gazing up into heaven? This same Jesus, who was taken up from you into heaven, will so come in like manner as you saw Him go into heaven." Acts 1:9-11.

One significant difference in the above scripture is that it features only two angels and a group of disciples.

When Christ returns, all the holy angels will be with him, all the saints will be with him, and every eye shall see Him. This is a worldwide event for all nations, cities, towns, villages, and tribes to witness.

There are many other promises in the Bible, but let me share two that are two-fold: a day of great joy for those Christians who are ready, but a day of judgment and destruction for those who have rejected such a great salvation offered to them through the gospel of Christ.

"When the Lord Jesus is revealed from heaven with his mighty angels, in flaming fire, taking vengeance on those who do not know God, and those who do not obey the gospel of our Lord Jesus Christ. These shall be punished with everlasting destruction from the presence of the Lord and from the glory of His power; when He comes in that day, to be glorified in His saints and to be admired among all those who believe; because our testimony among you was believed" (2 Thessalonians 1:7-10).

The apostle Peter confirms this two-fold promise of a day of judgment at the return of Christ.

"But the day of the Lord will come as a thief in the night, in which the heavens will pass away with a great noise, and the elements will melt with fervent heat; both the earth and the works that are in it will be burned up. Therefore, since all these things will be dissolved, what manner of persons ought you to be, in holy conduct and godliness, looking for and hastening the coming day of God? (2 Peter 3:10-12).

The world throughout the ages leading up to this conflict is still racked with war, lust, greed and death.

Our hopes for a better world, driven by the development of modern technology and advances in science and medicine, are a temporary solution that only covers the effects of corruption and sin, providing temporary relief until the next thing that throws the world into turmoil, as the human race rushes toward the next climatic event. If it were not for our depraved, sinful human nature, we might have some hope of arriving at a solution.

In his book *Hopeless – Yet There Is Hope*, Arno C. Gaebelein concludes with this prayer: "Even so come. Thou, hope of the hopeless, Thou, hope of Israel, Thou, hope of the world, all nations and creation, even so, come Lord Jesus."

He believes, as I do, that the ultimate solution to the world's conflicts will be resolved once and for all at the coming of Christ.

The question is, will humanity destroy itself while we wait? How long can we last? Time may be running out? Like the little girl who heard the clock strike thirteen times, she came running to her mother saying, "Is it later than you think?"

Why is it taking so long?

For centuries, Christians have asked, "Why is it taking so long for the promise of His coming to be fulfilled?" Many Christians have expressed frustration and disappointment that Christ has not yet returned.

It's not very pleasant when something isn't delivered as promised. The first house we ever built was in Melbourne. As you can imagine, we were very excited. We were promised it would take no longer than six months; it ended up being eighteen months before we could move in. In the meantime, we were paying extra rent and became very disappointed, angry and upset. The builder was full of flimsy excuses.

"Knowing this first: that scoffers will come in the last days, walking according to their own lusts, and saying, "Where is the promise of His coming? For since the fathers fell asleep, all things continue as they were from the beginning of creation." 2 Peter 3:3-4.

In the last days, scoffers will come questioning why the promise of His return is taking so long. This is evident in certain circles today. Sometimes, it is an excuse to cast off restraint, allowing them to live in a state of sin. Peter addresses this issue and provides a plausible reason for the delay.

"But beloved, do not forget this one thing, that with the Lord one day is as a thousand years, and a thousand years as one day. The Lord is not slack concerning His promise, as some count slackness, but is long-suffering toward us, not willing that any should perish but that all should come to repentance" 2 Peter 3:8-9.

In the above verses, we see a few essential things we need to understand –

- *God's timing and agenda are different to ours.*
- *God is patient and merciful to all.*
- *God's desire for all to repent.*
- *Our urgent need to evangelise.*
- *Christ will eventually return.*

What role will angels have at His coming

Apart from accompanying Jesus on his return, the angels will have several roles to fulfil.

Angels will gather the elect –

They will be responsible for gathering believers to Christ at His return.

"Then the sign of the Son of Man will appear in heaven, then all the tribes of the earth shall mourn, and they will see the Son of Man

coming on the clouds of heaven with power and great glory...And He will send His angels with a great sound of a trumpet, and they will gather His elect from the four winds, from one end of heaven to the other." Matthew 24:30-31.

The sign of the Son of Man mentioned above is a matter of debate. However, many scholars seem to believe it is a sign that illuminates the heavens with His glory, enabling every eye to see Him as He comes.

Angels will separate the righteous from the wicked –

They will be involved in the final separation of the righteous and the wicked. When my son Andrew and I go fishing, he always insists on casting a net into the water to see if he can get some bait fish.

"Again, the kingdom of heaven is like a dragnet that was cast into the sea and gathered some of every kind, which, when it was full, they drew to shore, and they sat down and gathered the good into vessels but threw the bad away. So, it will be at the end of the age. The angels will come forth, separate the wicked from among the just, and cast them into the furnace of fire. There will be wailing and gnashing of teeth." Matthew 13:47-50.

In *Systematic Theology*, Wayne Grudem states, "When Christ returns, the heavenly hosts will accompany Him, their radiant presence testifying to the divine majesty and power of the returning King." The angels will be the agents of divine judgment, separating the righteous from the wicked, gathering the elect to Himself, and carrying out the commands of the sovereign Lord."

Just how angels will be able to do this remains a mystery

Angels will judge those who disobey the gospel –

They will judge those who do not know God and are disobedient to the gospel of Christ.

"When the Lord Jesus is revealed from heaven with His mighty angels, in flaming fire taking vengeance on those who do not know God, and on those who do not obey the gospel of our Lord Jesus Christ." 2 Thessalonians 1:7-8.

What will the future look like for angels?

There appears to be no direct prophetic insight into the future regarding angels, other than what has already been revealed.

So, this will be more of a summary than a prediction of the future for angels.

- They will continue to walk among us as ministering spirits (sometimes as strangers) sent to minister to those who will inherit salvation.
- They will be involved in world events, playing crucial roles in end-times events and engaging in spiritual battles against demonic forces.
- They will accompany Christ at His return and gather the elect of God, separating the sheep from the goats.
- They will be involved in judging those who do not know God and the ungodly who have rejected the gospel.
- They will be involved in the final judgment of Satan and the fallen angels.
- They will worship and serve God around His throne, giving glory and honour to the slain Lamb of God.

- They will serve God and accompany the redeemed in some capacity throughout eternity.

What will your future look like?

When the angels accompany Christ on His return and fulfil their responsibility of gathering out of His kingdom all things that offend and work iniquity, it is hard to imagine what that will look like.

When God removes the devil and his work on earth, when sin is eliminated, and Christ sits on the throne. We are ushered eternally into a New Heaven and a New Earth, and the New Jerusalem descends from heaven to this earth, which will be filled with love, peace, and joy. We will be smitten by the tranquillity of it all. Redeemed man will be above the angels – Wow, what a future! I elaborate on some of these things in my book, *"The Ambiguous Kingdom."*

Considering today's unpredictability, believing all this is possible is hard. It takes a lot of faith to visualise the peace and serenity of an earth where Christ rules and reigns. However, there is no other solution or hope for humanity.

Today, you have a unique opportunity to choose; it will be too late when Christ returns. If you have not done so, you can cause the angels to rejoice in heaven by committing your life to Christ.

"Whoever confesses Me before men, him the Son of Man (Jesus) also will confess before the angels of God." Luke 12:8.

If you have never confessed Christ as your Saviour, you can right now. Put your faith and trust in Jesus Christ. You will be saved and receive eternal life if you believe in Him.

It is your choice; you have nothing to lose. It will be the wisest decision you have ever made in your life. Do not hesitate. Pray now, ask Jesus to forgive you, and confess Him as your Lord and Saviour.

"And behold I am coming quickly, and My reward is with Me, to give to every one according to his work." "I am the Alpha and the Omega, The Beginning and the End, the First and the Last." Revelation 22:12-13.

www.ingramcontent.com/pod-product-compliance
Lightning Source LLC
Chambersburg PA
CBHW022334300426
44109CB00040B/558